HARD TO HEART

HOW BOXER TIM BRADLEY WON CHAMPIONSHIPS AND RESPECT

BY BILL DWYRE

BACK STORY PUBLISHING, LLC
www.backstorypublishing.com

Hard to Heart
How Boxer Tim Bradley Won Championships and Respect
by Bill Dwyre

Copyright © 2017 by Back Story Publishing, LLC

All rights reserved. No part of this book may be reproduced, scanned, or stored in any printed, mechanical, or electronic form, or distributed or held or stored for distribution by any physical or electronic means, without written permission from Back Story Publishing. Please respect the rights of authors and publishers, and refrain from piracy of copyrighted materials. Thank you.

ISBN: 978-0-9993967-0-4
Library of Congress Control Number: 2017954224

Paperback editions printed in the United States of America.
For information on quantity discounts or special editions to
be used for educational programs, fundraising, premiums,
or sales promotions, please inquire via electronic mail at
admin@BackStoryPublishing.com, or write to Back Story Publishing,
Post Office Box 2580, Rancho Mirage, California 92270 USA.

News media inquiries may be directed to
newsroom@BackStoryPublishing.com

Credits
Cover photograph copyright © Chris Farina / ChrisFarina.com
Back cover photograph courtesy the Bradley Family and
copyright © Bradley Family photo

Designer: Stuart Funk
Back Story Publishing Editorial Director: Ellen Alperstein
www.BackStoryPublishing.com

INTRODUCTION

THIS IS A STORY about someone you probably never heard of who became famous playing a sport you probably don't like.

Why in the world would you read a book about someone you probably don't care about?

You would because this someone is Tim Bradley, a boy who found something he loved that was really hard to do. Tim Bradley grew up in a desert town where he was far more likely to fight his way into jail than into fame and fortune. Tim Bradley got bullied and thrown out of school. But he also became a five-time world-champion boxer.

Along the way, Tim learned how to care about other people, and when you make your living hitting guys with your fists, that's a good story.

Maybe you want to be a soccer player. Maybe you want to teach science, or be a rapper. It doesn't matter what you want to do. It matters that you figure out how to be happy while you're trying to do it, and how to treat other people along the way.

This year, Tim Bradley decided to retire from boxing. It was a really hard decision, because he's still a great athlete. "I still have the fire," he says, "but the fire is with my kids."

I'm a sportswriter. A couple of years ago, I was about to retire from a newspaper where I had worked for 35 years. I wrote a lot about boxing. Some of my stories were not very nice to the sport, or to Tim. My last assignment was to write about what turned out to be one of Tim's last fights. It was for a championship. The week of a big fight, most boxers rest. They hide with their friends and family, away from reporters and fans. But that week before Tim's big fight, he came into the press room. He had heard that I was retiring from the newspaper, and he wanted to say goodbye and to congratulate me on my long newspaper career.

That was just one of the reasons I knew I had to write Tim's story. I wanted to show how he went from being a small, black kid living among gang-bangers to a rich, famous jock whose real wealth is his heart of gold. Now he's saying goodbye to boxing, and hello to whatever comes next.

Bill Dwyre

1
NEAT LAWNS AND LOTS OF DIRT

FROM A VERY YOUNG AGE, Tim Bradley was feisty. "I had 100 fights in second grade," Tim says today, in 2017. He's 34 years old.

He grew up in a rough neighborhood in Palm Springs, California. Some people would be surprised that there are neighborhoods like that in Palm Springs, a desert city known for its resorts. It has a lot of rich residents and a lot of them are famous.

Palm Springs, and the larger Coachella Valley where it is located, is famous for golf and tennis. Those expensive sports are played there in winter, when much of the rest of the United States is cold and snowy. But in the part of town where Tim grew up, there were more people in youth gangs than there were people who played golf.

"I had a temper," Tim remembers. "I grew up in a tough neighborhood, and I was always one of the smallest guys. Other boys tried to bully me. I was always shorter. I always had a chip on my shoulder. All you had to do was look at me the wrong way.

"I would always resort to violence."

But Tim learned how to use that anger in a positive way. Eventually, he would become one of the greatest professional boxers in the world.

Less than a mile from where Tim grew up, tall turbines spin in the wind, making clean energy. You see thousands of them as you enter the Coachella Valley minutes from the house where young Tim lived. His parents still live there.

Today, it's a mixed neighborhood. There are nice homes with neat lawns. There are scrubby fields, and lots of dirt. New cars are parked in front of some homes; at others, rusty cars with missing wheels are perched on cement blocks. A couple of churches are nearby, and a gas station/mini-mart.

A few blocks from the Bradley house is a park and recreation center. A mural painted on the playground wall shows children — black, brown, and white — playing.

Tim's father, Ray, moved there in 1981. "I met Kathleen at the park," Ray says, referring to his wife. They have been married almost 36 years.

Ray is muscular. He's 5 feet 7 inches tall and weighs 226 pounds. When he was young, Ray wanted to be a bodybuilder, and today, as a security guard at a local high school, he still works out.

Kathleen, who often is called "Kathy," says that she and her husband have "always been tempted" to move out of the neighborhood.

"I hear about home invasions, but the gangs don't bother us," she says.

Ray adds, "They leave us alone. They know who I am. They respect me for what I do."

As Tim became one of the famous people who live in the valley, a lot of people came to respect Ray and Kathy Bradley for how they raised him. For how they helped an angry kid who talked with his fists become not only a world-class boxer, but a nice person and a good father. Tim, who is married to a woman named Monica, is the father of three children and the stepfather of two. Today, the family of seven lives in the wealthy city of Rancho Mirage, 15 minutes away from his parents.

2
A LITTLE MONSTER

TIM WAS EXPELLED from one school when he was in second grade. That was the year he said he fought 100 times. He was expelled from another school when he was in fourth grade because of what happened on a school bus.

Tim's sister Shantae is one year older than he. Tim has another sister two years younger. Her name is Myechia. When he was expelled and bused to a different school about 10 miles away, his sisters went with him to that school.

"There was lots of racial tension there," Tim says. "The kids were mostly Latino. My sisters and I were three of maybe seven blacks in the school. Right away, they started calling us 'monkeys.'"

If you are black, this is a serious insult based on the

color of your skin.

Tim's trouble here began on the playground. One day, one of his sisters playing there said one boy had called her a "monkey." Tim hit him.

"I'd always confronted them with my fists," Tim says. "I was never much of a talker. I didn't care how big they were. I was never afraid of anybody. That's just the way I was."

Another time, his sister told him somebody had spit in her mouth.

"I confronted him," Tim says. "Then we had a few words, I hit him, and spit in *his* mouth. I got sent to the office, but I didn't care.... I never thought about consequences. The only thing in my mind was protecting my sisters."

Tim, right, is the middle child. He always protected his sisters, Katherine Myechia, the baby, and big sister Shantae Latrice.

Soon, there was another incident on the playground. Tim got into an argument with another boy, and, as a fight was about to break out, somebody warned Tim that this boy knew karate.

"He came at me with all that karate stuff," Tim says, "and I just hit him with one straight shot, in the eye. That was the end of the fight. But it was school picture day and he had to have his picture taken with a black eye. I kind of liked that."

But the adults at the school didn't. Tim got suspended for three days.

Then he got into the fight on the school bus.

"I got on the bus and sat in a seat that I knew I shouldn't have," Tim recalls. "That seat was where a fifth-grader always sat. He got on, told me to move, and told me if I didn't, he would 'choke me out.' I didn't move and he grabbed me and started choking me. He was much bigger than I was. It wasn't really a big fight. I couldn't do much.

"The bus driver pulled him off me. I'm glad he did, because the kid might have killed me. I remember the bus driver telling me that my dad ought to teach me how to fight better. That really made my dad angry when I told him."

After the bus driver reported the fight, Tim was expelled.

"My dad went to the school principal and the principal told him what a bad kid I was. My dad asked the

Tim's father, Ray, at home on the lawn Tim used to mow as one of his chores.

principal how he would feel if somebody choked him out. My dad told him he didn't care for what the bus driver had said.

"It didn't matter. He threw both my dad and me out of his office. I got expelled and the other kid stayed."

Tim was sent to another school closer to home. His father, Ray, worked for that school district and this school was Tim's last chance.

"I got a lot of passes because of my dad, because he worked for the school district," Tim says. But he also got punished by his parents when he let himself lose control too much. They thought there had to be consequences for behaving badly. In the Bradley house, that meant losing privileges like playing Nintendo, doing more chores, and getting grounded.

At this school, Tim remembers that his dad told him that "this would be my last chance, that there would be no other school that would take me if I got into another fight. The teachers really started to keep me under control. They were always watching me.

"I knew I had to change. I knew that my way of thinking was the wrong way. I knew that I had a thug mentality. That's what I called it. I was pretty much a little monster. My dad told me that he did not raise me to be a bully."

Even if he shaped up at school, Tim still had a lot to overcome because his new school, closer to his home, was dangerous. The main gang in his neighborhood was known as GWPC, the Gateway Posse Crips.

"My uncles and cousins were involved with the gangs," Tim says. "I was drawn to that. You see your friends, and their fathers and mothers always had nice cars. I could go to my uncles or cousins and they would have big wads of cash. As a kid, you don't know any better.

"I wanted to be part of it. I wanted to do what they did. I'd get on the school bus and sack down my pants, just like the gang guys."

Ray Bradley wanted no part of it. He was not involved with gangs and he demanded the same of his children. Tim says he knew how harshly he would be punished if he ever hooked up with a gang. He also says that his dad was his hero.

Ray and Kathleen had lots of rules. Their children were allowed to go to the park and the recreation center, but only during daylight. Another rule was that Tim, who loved to fight, was not allowed to participate in the sport of boxing. He kept pestering his parents to let him try it, but Ray and Kathy didn't like the sport, didn't like its violence. It would be no fun, Kathy says, to watch her boy get hit in the face.

3
FINDING HEAVEN

TO THIS DAY, RAY BRADLEY isn't quite sure how Tim talked him into letting him try boxing. Even though Ray has always been athletic and fit, he, like Kathleen, didn't like the idea of his son getting hit in the face.

"When my dad came to California," Tim says, "it was his goal to become a professional bodybuilder. But then, when he got around all the other bodybuilders and realized he would have to take all those drugs to keep up, he backed off. It wasn't worth it to him what the drugs would do to his body."

Ray remembers how the "sport" of bodybuilding — practicing certain kinds of weightlifting routines in order to shape your muscles a certain way to please the judges and audience in a competition — had become spoiled. Too many competitors were taking drugs to help their bodies do what nature and hard work couldn't.

"It was hard finding a job," he says. "I wanted to make a living as a bodybuilder. But when I found out what drugs you needed to take, I just wouldn't do it. I figured I would be a vegetable by the time I was 50."

By being a "vegetable," Ray is talking about one of the serious health problems caused by the drugs some bodybuilders take — damage to their hearts and to their ability to think.

Over the years, Ray held several jobs for the school system, but mostly he was a security guard. That was his job when Tim was in fifth grade, and had made a new friend at school. His name was Julio, and he practiced boxing in a gym near the school. Tim and Julio would goof around, slapping boxing gloves against each other,

When he started training at the Palm Springs Boxing Club, 10-year-old Tim was smaller than the heavy bag.

but Tim was not allowed to go into the boxing gym.

"I told him to tell Julio he couldn't box," Ray says.

But Tim persisted. He wanted to get into a boxing ring.

Finally, he wore down his dad. One day after work, Ray told Tim that he would take him to the gym. "I don't know why I changed my mind," Ray says. "I think I had a good day at work and was feeling good. I didn't have to arrest anybody. Maybe that was it. Something just came over me."

It was 1993. Fifteen years later, in 2008, Tim Bradley would be a major world boxing champion. Between 2005 and 2008 Tim had won two World Youth Championships. They were meaningful, but not high profile or well-paid.

"We walked in the door," Ray says, remembering that first day, "and some old guy meets us there. His name was O.J. Couture and he ran the gym, the Palm Springs Boxing Club. Tim shook his hand and this O.J. says, 'Wow.' Then he looks at me and says, 'This kid is gonna be a world champ.'"

Tim remembers that moment, too.

"My dad didn't like that," he says. "He told the guy he didn't need to be sold. We were there to sign up."

Ray remembers something else. "For some reason," he says, "I kind of believed this guy."

Coaches and boxers at the Palm Springs Boxing Club. Tim is the second boxer from the left.

Tim describes O.J., who died several years ago, as a man in his 70s, a "real straight-shooter," with a Boston accent, curly blond hair, and a "big old pot belly."

Ray told Tim that "I would tell him if he had no talent. I grew up watching boxing on TV all the time. I knew the sport."

Tim was thrilled.

"I loved it, right away," he says. "I walked in that gym and saw all those posters on the wall. Pictures of Muhammad Ali, Sugar Ray Leonard. And all those green championship belts they had. I wanted one of those.

Right away, I wanted one. I looked around and there was the speed bag, and a heavy bag. I was 10 years old. I really didn't know what they were. But I was in heaven."

In no time Tim learned how to use all the different pieces of equipment in the gym. It was as if boxing fed a hunger he couldn't satisfy any other way.

"I would sit in class and think about boxing," Tim says. "I'd get up in the morning and that would be the first thing on my mind. It took over my life."

Ten-year-old Tim weighed 72 pounds when he checked in at O.J.'s gym. O.J. told him he would need to get into boxing shape before he could get in a boxing ring against an opponent. They told him that would take at least two weeks.

By middle school, Tim was boxing every weekend in tournaments. He often won trophies and medals.

Not for Tim. He had been working out with his dad since he was little. The trainers asked him to do pull-ups and sit-ups, and to toss around a medicine ball, which is a heavy, solid mass more like a round sack of potatoes than a ball.

He did it all. It was easy.

"I could do more pull-ups than anybody else in the gym," Tim says. Some gym members were as old as 21.

In three days Tim was in the ring. His opponent was his friend, Julio.

"I only knew one punch," Tim says. "I only knew the jab."

Boxing often is called "the sweet science." That's because the best boxers use a wide variety of punches, and they know when to use which punch — the strategy part of boxing combined with the athletic skill is the "science."

Boxing "science" class is held in the gym, where young fighters wear headgear to protect their heads against punches and falls. Professional boxers — people who fight for money — and male boxers in the Olympic Games fight without headgear. But every boxer wears it during practice in the ring, which is called "sparring."

The main punch boxers learn is the jab. If you're right-handed, a jab is a quick left-handed thrust; if you're left-handed, the thrust comes from the right. Tim quickly learned that the purpose of a jab is to test the opponent, to soften him up for a harder punch from the fighter's stronger hand from a trickier angle. A great jab lands often. It scores lots of points with judges who award points based on how many punches you land. Tim soon understood that the jab is useful, but it seldom knocks out the other boxer.

Throwing a punch with a straight right or left hand is more powerful than the compact jab. A straight punch lands harder than a jab.

Another punch is a hook, which means the elbow is held away from the body when the punch is thrown toward either the side of an opponent's body or his head. An uppercut is like a hook, except the elbow is held close to the body and usually the fist is aimed at the opponent's jaw.

All of this was new to Tim.

Julio had been training at the gym for two or three months when Tim first joined him in the ring. Almost 25 years later, Tim still remembers exactly what happened:

"First thing, Julio hits me with a shot ... then he hits me in the nose with another. BOOM ... hits me again ... hurts me ... I'm teary-eyed, I'm getting mad."

When the match was over, Tim sat, defeated, on the edge of the ring with a busted lip and a bloody nose. In the next 20 years or so, he would almost never lose.

"My dad came over and said, 'You done? You quit? I told you this sport is tough.'"

Tim was not done. He just wanted to get tougher.

To do that, Tim would have to do work harder than

he ever had. The very next day, Ray got him up at 5 a.m. From then on, into his teenage years, Tim Bradley was often seen by early risers on the west side of Palm Springs. He was often spotted jogging up the steep road to where the famous Palm Springs Aerial Tramway took passengers high up Mt. San Jacinto overlooking the city.

"He'd put the flashing lights on in the car, turned music up on the radio," Tim says of his dad's training routine, "and followed me as I jogged. When people honked, he'd just motion them to go around."

Tim started fighting as an amateur — someone who competes, but not for pay — and boxing would take him and his family on hundreds of weekend trips to hundreds of tournaments. But first, he had to take care of one thing.

"I got to fight Julio again," says Tim.

He had learned fast.

"I won. I made him cry."

His early bouts with Julio started a habit Tim still has — loyalty.

"I talked to Julio last year," Tim says. "He lives in Los Angeles and has three kids."

4

LIVING ON TROPHIES

SOON, LIFE WAS PULLING from all directions at young Tim Bradley. By the time he was 12, he was boxing in an amateur tournament almost every weekend. The family usually went along.

"Lots of miles traveled," says Tim's mom, Kathleen.

The first weekend he competed, he was named "Fighter of the Tournament" for O.J. Couture's Palm Springs Boxing Club. He would go on to win Junior Olympic titles six times. He never lost a Junior Olympics match.

Tim Bradley was turning heads.

"I was so nervous that first weekend," Tim says. "I couldn't eat. I remember walking into the gym and looking around at all those other kids and wondering which one I would box."

> **HE'S GOT A FIGHTING CHANCE**
> # Closing on a dream
> **Cathedral City's Bradley sets sights on Olympics**
>
> By Ed Castro
> THE DESERT SUN
>
> **CATHEDRAL CITY** — Step by step, Timothy Bradley is getting what he wants.
> With every district title and with every national championship, Bradley gets closer to a shot at realizing his dream.
> The amateur boxer from Cathedral City has his sights set on the 2004 summer Olympics.
> His latest achievement moved him closer to a shot at ... ing for Team ...

© THE DESERT SUN

At one early tournament, an elderly gentleman asked Ray if Tim was his son. Ray nodded and the man said, "That boy is going to be more famous than Muhammad Ali." That was the second time someone's first look at Tim drew such a high compliment. And for the second time, Ray says now, "For some reason, I believed him. I got chills up and down my spine."

Another gym old-timer watched Tim once and told his dad, "Your son has a jab like Larry Holmes." Holmes was a former world heavyweight champion.

Among the few losses Tim suffered in his amateur career were to Andre Berto, who became welterweight champion in 2008 and 2011. But Tim would also hold those 147-pound titles at different times.

"I don't want this to sound like an excuse," Ray says, "but both times he fought Berto, Tim was injured. I remember one time, he had an injured knuckle."

Tim never fought Berto as a professional.

Boxers always fight someone of a similar size because being five or six pounds heavier than someone can be an unfair advantage. So boxing is divided into weight classes, which is why there are so many divisions in the sport. As a professional, Tim often would fight weighing 147 pounds — in the welterweight division. It's only seven pounds more than the super lightweight class, 140 pounds, where Tim started. The class above welterweight, 154 pounds, is the super welterweight division. And the one right below 140 pounds is 135 pounds — lightweight. Professional boxing has 18 weight classes, ranging from light minimumweight (as high as 102 pounds) to heavyweight, which has no upper weight limit.

Just as boxing requires strategy in the ring, sometimes "making weight" is strategic — a boxer wants to get as close as possible to the maximum weight of the class without going over. A lot of boxers have a difficult time staying strong when they have to lose pounds quickly to qualify for a certain division.

But even when he was young, Tim never had a problem making weight.

"Medical Romance"
CCHS Winter Ball 2000-2001

As a senior at Cathedral City High School, Tim was King of the Winter Ball.

"Tim didn't lose many matches. He was just magic in the ring," Ray says. "One of the reasons was that you never knew when he was hurt. I told him, never show that you are hurt when you are in the ring. You can do all the screaming you want, once you get to the locker room."

Tim followed that valuable advice his whole career. It was a key part of his boxing strategy.

"I remember one fight when he had his eye grazed," Ray explains. "I remember his coach in the corner yelling at him, 'Hit the guy in the middle.'"

What was he talking about? It turns out that Tim's eye was so injured that the other fighter looked like three guys. But, Ray says, "He didn't tell us about his eye until he got done and he had won the fight. We didn't even know, because he always kept everything to himself in the ring."

Tim was a great fighter as a kid, but Tim was also a kid. He lost one fight the night after his dad had nagged him to get to bed early. Tim stayed up until midnight.

"He went out and lost because he was tired," Ray said. "That was a lesson learned."

He was taught another lesson by his mom.

"When he got to middle school," Kathleen says, "he discovered girls. His grades went from A's to F's."

Just as he got punished when he got into too many fights when he was 8, there were consequences when Tim was 12 and did poorly in school. His parents knew he had the ability to be a good student. So, Kathleen reports, "We took him out of boxing for two months. We put him in the kitchen, washing dishes. Once those two months were over and he got back into the gym, you couldn't have

Tim prepared for a bout as a high school student and member of Team USA at a tournament in France.

seen a happier kid. After that, grades were no problem."

It wasn't just Tim's parents who had him on a short leash; O.J. had rules at the boxing gym, too.

"He had three things," Tim says. "Number 1, you could not get in fights at school. Number 2, you had to bring academic reports to the gym. Bad grades and you couldn't box. Number 3, if you were in any sort of trouble, he would actually go and visit your teachers."

For Tim, fighting in school was no longer a problem. The 100 fights he got into as a second-grader became zero fights as a middle-schooler.

"I'd see a fight and I'd walk away," Tim says. "With my father, or O.J., I had to fly straight. I also was starting to realize that I could hurt somebody badly. My hands were weapons."

He's not exaggerating. Tim's muscular body was a weapon. He wasn't going to be a big guy — he would grow to be 5-feet 6 inches tall — but his athletic abilities were huge.

"A lot of the coaches at Cathedral City High School were really mad at me," Ray says of the school Tim attended and where Ray still works as a security guard. "They still are. They wanted Tim to play football. They said he was one of those kids who loves to hit, and that's exactly what they needed. But I wouldn't let him play. I told him that if he was going to spend this much time in boxing, we weren't going to wreck all that by risking a football injury."

Of course, that's not what Tim wanted to hear. He knew he could be a good football defensive back at Cathedral City. He was very competitive in everything he did, especially sports.

"If I wasn't first," he says, "I had to be second. If not second, third. I've always been like that."

The problem was that boxing was not played as a high school sport. So, Tim's high school sports career focused on track. He ran races from the 440 to the mile.

"My day went like this," he recalls. "Up at 5 a.m. to run in the street. Back home and off to school. After school, track practice for two hours, then after track, over to the boxing gym."

Kathleen and Tim Bradley, bundled up against the cold weather in Northern Michigan.

Still, he was able to maintain a 3.0 grade point average, and he enjoyed his favorite subjects, math and science.

"I was never a big book reader," he says, "But if I saw a book about a sports hero of mine, like Muhammad Ali or Michael Jordan, I couldn't put it down."

He had made such an impression in his weekend boxing tournaments that he got a scholarship to Northern Michigan University. At the time, and until recently, it had a training program where potential Olympic boxers went to school and also trained with some of the best fighters in the country.

So Tim moved from one of the hottest climates in the country to one of the coldest. While he was there, he won a Golden Gloves tournament.

He also got very cold.

"He wrote home one time," Ray remembers, "and told us it was so cold that the lake [Lake Superior] freezes over up there."

For somebody from Alaska, that's not a big deal. For Tim Bradley, from the hot desert, it was. After two years, it was time to come home. He hadn't made an Olympic team at Northern Michigan, but his boxing career was promising.

He wasn't home too long before he told his dad it was time to move from fighting as an amateur to fighting as a professional. He was 20 years old.

"He said," Ray remembers, "that you can't live on trophies."

5

THE LUCK OF LOVE

GOOD PROFESSIONAL BOXERS have a whole team of people helping with their careers. Tim had to learn how to put together a good team.

A prizefighter's team includes a promoter, with whom he signs a contract giving that company the right to decide whom he fights, when, and where. The idea is that the boxer gives up some control in exchange for more and better opportunities. The main person who had this control for Tim had always been his dad, Ray. But a promoter not only lines up opponents, it rents gyms or arenas where the fight will be held. It also sets the amount of money the fighter will get. That pay is called the boxer's purse.

Also on the team is a manager, who handles the box-

In 2005, Tim still wasn't earning big paychecks. But he was becoming well-known as The Desert Storm, and he knocked down Juan Yoani Cervantes for his eighth win and a junior world championship. One month later, in September 2005, he won his first youth world championship.

er's personal business affairs, such as making travel arrangements, ordering equipment, and paying bills. Two key duties the manager has are to negotiate with the promoter for the best deal for the boxer, and to hire the trainer, who is the boxer's coach. The coach plans the workouts to make sure the boxer is in peak condition leading up to the fight. He also helps with fight strategy. During the fight, he gives instructions between rounds when the fighter is resting in his corner.

Also in the corner on fight night is a cut man, whose job is pretty much just that — he treats the cuts a fighter gets during the round to protect him as much as possible for the next round. In Tim's corner for every single fight was his dad. He advised, applied bags of ice, and did whatever else was needed to keep Tim strong during a fight.

Tim had decided to be become a serious professional, but he still liked to have fun. One night, he was at a party with some friends. All of them knew that Tim was struggling, and needed somebody to promote his fights. Somebody in Tim's group spotted a bunch of people across the room, including the son of boxing promoter Ken Thompson. The groups moved together. They talked a little smack. Somebody challenged Tim: "Let's see what you've got."

Suddenly, somebody slapped Tim in the face. He responded with an open-handed slap. Angry words were exchanged before things cooled down. By the end of the night, Tim had the phone number for Thompson Boxing. Not long after, Thompson promoted Tim's first pro fight — he had taken a party scuffle into a real business relationship.

Tim made his professional boxing debut in August 2004. Nine days later, he turned 21.

Because he was from the desert and was known for

the flurry of punches he threw, the nickname "Desert Storm" gradually became a natural for the boxing media.

Unless you are an Olympic champion, nothing comes easy in the early years of being a pro fighter. His first prizefight was about 80 miles away from Palm Springs, at the Omega Products International in Corona, California. It was more a warehouse than a gymnasium. It certainly was not an arena. His next five fights were in the ballroom of a DoubleTree Hotel. It was right next to the airport in Ontario, about an hour's drive west of Palm Springs.

"For a long time," Tim says, "I had a lot of $800 work nights in hotel ballrooms."

His professional debut matched him in the ring with Francisco Martinez, who also was boxing professionally for the first time. Little did Martinez know that he was facing a guy who would not lose in his next 30 fights.

Thompson Boxing promoted Tim's fights for four years. During that time, Tim was seldom tested in the ring. It was low pay and less prestige. Ray Bradley says that they were treated well and they loved the Thompson slogan: "Path to Glory." It describes perfectly what Thompson had been for Tim.

As Tim's career grew, so did the team supporting him, in and out of the ring. When he was 25, he got a new promoter, Gary Shaw Promotions. The quality of the matches and the money were inching up.

As Grand Marshal of the Palm Springs parade celebrating Black History Month in 2006, Tim signed autographs and shared the youth championship belt and medal with kids from his hometown.

Luck found Tim again. This time, it was the luck of love.

Tim had known Monica Manzo since grade school. She was two years older, so they were just casual friends who had gone to Cathedral City High School at the same time. A few years later, because of boxing, everybody knew who Tim was. But Tim knew who Monica was, too.

"I remember what a good soccer player she was," he says. "And tough, always the one getting the yellow and red cards. I liked that. I also remember what beautiful legs she had."

After high school, they had gone their separate ways. At 18, Monica had married Erik Smoot. He went into the Navy, she went with him, and when they got out, their first child, Robert, was two years old. Five years later, the Smoots had their second child, Alaysia. Two years after that, they were divorced.

"I just got married too young," Monica explains now.

By the time she was 25, Monica had two children and was working at two jobs to pay for the house she had bought. Tim, 23, was still fighting mostly low-paying matches. To boost his boxing income, he washed dishes at a Coco's Bakery Restaurant, then he took a better job as a waiter at another restaurant, Mimi's Cafe.

"I had moved from the back of the room to the front of the room," Tim jokes.

One day at Mimi's, Tim spotted Monica in a back booth, eating with a friend.

Tim walked over and said, "Scoot over."

Today, Monica remembers, "We had a longer conversation that day than ever before."

The romance had begun.

During the day, Monica worked as a secretary at Cathedral City High School. At night, she taught parenting classes.

"My parents lived close by," she says, "and we ate a lot of meals there."

Because she and Tim were at such different places in life, she had trouble seeing them as a couple. "I told him," she says, "'I have responsibilities, I have two kids and a mortgage. You can just party.'"

Tim's dad Ray knew Monica well. He saw her every day at Cathedral City High. When he heard that Tim had become re-acquainted with her, he started singing her praises to his son. Tim started showing up at school. He asked Monica for her phone number. She said no. He gave her his. She never called. She assumed Tim had a girlfriend. He eventually told her he didn't.

They started dating. Then she hurt her knee and needed surgery. She was a single mom with two little kids at home, working two jobs, and hobbling around on a bum knee.

"Tim stepped right in," she says. "He took over, fixing meals and everything. He even did the laundry. You'll never see *my* dad do laundry."

Monica was impressed by Tim's sense of responsibility even though she was troubled by his career choice — boxing. But it was his life, his work, and she wanted to support the thing he loved.

They were dating seriously by spring of 2008 when Tim had his biggest fight so far. The match against well-known Jose Luis Castillo would be in Mexico, and the winner would get to fight for the world 140-pound title.

"We got our airline tickets, and flew to Mexico," Monica says.

But Castillo couldn't make weight. When that happens, a few things can occur. If the fight had been for a title, the overweight fighter loses his chance. The fighter who made weight is awarded the title. No matter what kind of fight it is, for a title or not, the boxers' teams decide what to do. They might give the fighter who did make weight a bigger purse, and the one who didn't gets less. Sometimes the fight is simply called off.

Promoters hate it when boxers don't make weight. They've put out a lot of money, and at best, their "show" gets a black mark. At worst, it's canceled, and they lose money. If that happens, sometimes a promoter no longer will represent the fighter. So, many pro boxing careers have ended not in the ring, but on the scale.

It's unusual when the fighter who makes weight has to go home empty-handed. But that's what happened to Tim.

"So we just paid the hotel bill, got back on the plane, and came home," Monica says. "I thought that was really wrong. Nobody seemed to care. It was just the way boxing was."

It took a few years, but Monica eventually turned those feelings into actions. Eventually, she would take over as Tim's manager. By summer of 2013, she was negotiating with promoters for the amount of his purses, and making sure he was treated fairly. And she did it so well that in 2015 she was nominated by the Boxing Writers Association of America for a huge honor — manager of the year.

She did all this even though she disliked how her man made his living.

"I didn't have to like it," she says, "but I had to respect what he loved."

For years, she was in conflict with herself. She tried hard to get Tim the best boxing deals, and at the same time really wanted him to stop.

"I never told him it was time," she says, "because I thought it was time long ago."

6

CHAMPION OF THE WORLD

ONE GOOD THING came out of the canceled fight against Castillo, when the Mexican star didn't make weight and Tim and Monica returned home with nothing except travel bills. The good thing was that the fight was to have decided who would get the next shot at a World Boxing Council 140-pound title. Because Castillo was disqualified, Tim got that shot.

The World Boxing Council (WBC) is one of a few boxing groups that award championship titles. The other major ones are the World Boxing Association (WBA), the World Boxing Organization (WBO), and International Boxing Federation (IBF). They are called "sanctioning" organizations.

Each one has its own set of weight-division champions and its own rules of how its champions must defend

In the locker room after the fight against Junior Witter, Tim celebrated his first big-money victory in 2008. The WBC Super Lightweight title opened doors to high-profile matches and a big-time promoter.

their titles against challengers. All of these systems are designed so that lower-ranked fighters can work their way up. Each sanctioning group is paid a fee by promoters to help publicize title fights. The winners, in addition to the purses, receive fancy jeweled belts in the ring after their victory.

In May 2008, Tim challenged for the WBC super lightweight title. In 20 fights, he had never lost a professional bout. He had won world youth titles, but this was a much bigger bout. He was to fight champion Junior Witter in that fighter's hometown, Nottingham. That's in England, an expensive place to travel for a struggling boxer. Tim was becoming a well-known prizefighter, but his small purses didn't match his growing fame. He and Monica, who weren't married yet but lived together with the kids, still struggled to pay the bills. They both still worked several jobs.

Monica now understood Tim's passion for his sport. "I started to believe he would be the Tim Bradley he talked about being," she says. "He was so confident. At one point, he had me believing so much that I think I believed more than he did."

By early May, Tim had been in England for a week. Monica was supposed to fly in the night before the fight, but she was late and Tim couldn't reach her. Instead of focusing on his fight or resting, he worried about Monica.

When she finally arrived at 4:30 in the morning, she explained that her taxi driver had gotten lost on the way to the hotel.

The pressure was off, but only for a moment. Tim really needed to win this fight, Monica told him, because "our checkbook balance was $11."

All the money they had in the bank was $11! And soon, Monica's house payment was about to go up $1,000 each month. They had arrived home not long before to find an official note on their front door. It was an eviction notice — it said they had to catch up on the payments they owed, or move out of the house.

"We cried in bed that night," Tim says.

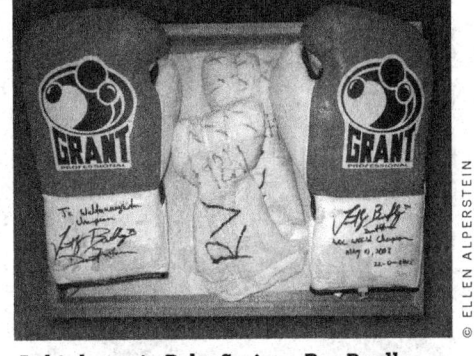

At his home in Palm Springs, Ray Bradley displays the hand wraps and gloves Tim wore in the fight against Junior Witter.

They managed to save the house that time, but the pressure to win this fight, and its purse, was high.

On fight night, Ray was in Tim's corner, as always. "I knew he was going to win. I never doubted," he says.

Tim felt the same way.

"I wasn't nervous," he says. "I knew what I had to do.

I was there to win. I was there to win that green belt. I remember that was the first thing I saw when I walked into O.J.'s gym, that green belt. Here I was, fighting for the WBC championship of the world."

His parents were there. Monica was there. And so, in spirit, was the late O.J. Couture. He was Tim's first real boxing trainer, the one who told Tim and Ray when they first walked into his gym almost 15 years earlier that one day Tim would be a world champion. O.J. wouldn't get to see his first try because he had died many years earlier.

By the time Tim was looking for a new promoter, he and Monica had married in the desert where they grew up. She was learning the business of boxing, and soon would become his manager.

"I remember his Coke-bottle glasses," Tim says. "I remember the day he weighed me, looked me up and down, felt my arm and my chest. Then he said, 'There is something about you. Just something about you. You're gonna be a champion.'"

Loyal Tim had saved a pair of O.J.'s hand wraps — the material boxers wind around their hands, under their boxing gloves. "I wore them that night," Tim says. "I remember my dad saying to me that O.J. was there with me, there to protect me.

"They were terrible hand wraps, the most horrible I had ever seen," Tim says now. "But I remember my dad saying that O.J. would be there with me, in the ring."

The bell rang, and the fight began. The home crowd was loud, rooting for Witter. But it was Tim who came out strong, and through the first half of a fight that could last for 12 rounds, he never let up. He even knocked Witter down in the sixth round. Not even English judges could give the fight to the boxer from their home country. Still, Tim won a split-decision victory — there were three judges, and one scored the fight as a victory for Witter.

The fight wasn't that close, but Tim didn't care. At 24 years old, he was a world boxing champion. He was a family provider. His winner's purse was $52,000, and the family checking account now held $52,011.

From then on, Tim Bradley's boxing matches would pay him at least $100,000. They would be held in bigger arenas and in bigger cities. After defending his WBC Super Lightweight title in Biloxi, Mississippi, Tim added a WBO Super Lightweight title in Montreal, Quebec, even though he got knocked down twice by Kendall Holt. In Rancho Mirage, at a well-known casino's boxing arena only a few miles from his house, he had a big fight against undefeated Lamont Peterson. When it was over, only Tim was undefeated.

As Tim's boxing fortunes increased, so did his love for Monica. In 2010, they were married.

In January 2011, Tim fought Devon Alexander in the Silverdome in Pontiac, Michigan. The huge arena had been the home of the Detroit Lions of the National Football League, and the Pistons of the National Basketball League. That night, it was Tim Bradley's house: He won after he hit his opponent's left eye so hard that Alexander couldn't see out of it. The ring doctor and the referee stopped the fight in the 10th round.

By now, everyone in boxing could see why Tim was special. One of his tools was, simply, being tough — Tim knew that if he didn't show he was hurt or in pain, other fighters couldn't sense that he might be weakening. Another of Tim's skills was speed. His hands and feet moved as fast as anybody's, except for maybe Floyd Mayweather Jr., who was famously quick in the ring. Like Mayweather, Tim seemed impossible to hit.

Ray Bradley explains how Tim developed his foot speed. "I used to tie his hands behind his back and have the younger guys get in the ring and try to hit him," he says. "They couldn't. He'd just duck and dance."

When you can't use your hands to protect yourself, Ray was thinking, you better find another way to escape.

Tim's next title defense was to be against Amir Khan of England. Tim was guaranteed $1.3 million for that fight. That's a huge amount of money, but Tim didn't think it was fair pay for how high he had soared. Only 2½ years earlier, the $52,000 he won for his first world championship had seemed like a pot of gold.

Because he refused to take the Khan fight, the WBC took away his title. His promoter, Gary Shaw, dropped him. People in boxing wondered if Tim — and Monica, although she wasn't yet officially his manager — knew what they were doing.

A year and a half later, in a packed house in one of the most famous venues for boxing, everybody knew they did.

7
THE LITTLE FISH

IN 2011, TIM BRADLEY entered the world of big-money boxing.

He had turned down Amir Khan, who had tried to sway Tim by offering him an equal split of the purse, even though Tim's status in the boxing world was lower than Khan's. He also had offered Tim a larger share of the pay-per-view money. Most of that would have come from British boxing fans who would pay their TV cable company a one-time fee to watch the match on their home TVs. Some reports said that the $1.3 million Tim was offered first had become $1.8 million

But Tim, and Cameron Dunkin, his manager at the time, had gambled. They turned it down, hoping for a bigger payday from another prizefight.

Tim's refusal to fight Khan left him looking for a new promoter. He had always talked about going with one of the best companies in the business, Top Rank Boxing, based in Las Vegas. It produced many of the top boxing matches in the world, and its Number 1 fighter was Manny Pacquiao. He, like Floyd Mayweather Jr., was one of the top boxers in the world, and Tim's goal was to challenge him in the ring. Such a fight was high status and it meant big money.

Top Rank was run by Bob Arum, the most famous boxing executive in the country. In his long career, he had promoted fights for Muhammad Ali as well as many of the stars who followed him, including Mayweather, Oscar de la Hoya, and Pacquiao.

Arum followed every part of boxing closely, even when it didn't directly involve his fighters. When Tim turned down the fight with Amir Khan, Arum sent Todd DuBoef, president of Top Rank, to talk to Tim.

"It isn't like we hadn't watched Bradley," Arum says. "We had seen lots of him. Lamont Peterson was our fighter when he fought Bradley.... We kind of expected Peterson to win, but Bradley handled him pretty well.

"Then I watched him fight, and beat, Devon Alexander. We were impressed."

DuBoef went to see Bradley with a powerful message.

"Todd told him that we would put him in the ring against Joel Casamayor," Arum says, "and if he won that match, we'd put him in against Manny Pacquiao."

Pacquiao, a wildly popular fighter from the Philippines, hadn't lost in 14 matches, since 2003. When you got into the ring with Pacquiao, you knew you were in for a night of speed and hard punches. You also knew you were in for a big payday. So Casamayor was a stepping stone for Tim.

He was also an opponent with an interesting story.

Casamayor had won a gold medal fighting at 118 pounds for Cuba in the 1992 Olympics. But as he trained for the next Olympics four years later, he realized he couldn't make that weight. His failure would be not only a huge disappointment in Cuba, it also could be a huge problem for Casamayor, because that country isn't as free as the U.S.

So, along with another fighter, in 1996 Casamayor defected — in other words, he left Cuba illegally — and came to the United States. Casamayor became one of Top Rank's boxers, even though Arum really had wanted the other guy who'd left Cuba, a famous heavyweight named Ramon Garbey.

"Before I knew it," Arum says, "there was this little fish who came along with the deal."

On Nov. 11, 2011, Tim defended his World Boxing

Organization title for the fourth time. He assumed it would be the last time he would fight at 140 pounds — after Casamayor, he would go up to 147 pounds, welterweight class, and stay there for many big fights.

For now, the 28-year-old world champion with a match record of 26-0, was up against the 40-year-old Casamayor, with a record of 38-6-1. Whoever won got Pacquiao, and the $5 million that came with it.

8
LUNCH PAIL TIM

TIM'S FIGHT against Joel Casamayor in 2011 was billed as part of the main event. Nobody was buying that. Including Tim.

Big fight nights always have more than one match. The main event on the boxing card — which is a list of all the matches that day — usually starts around 8:30 p.m. But the undercard fights — or less interesting bouts — start in late afternoon. They help promoters sell tickets to family and friends of those up-and-coming boxers, on top of the big money promoters hope to get from TV's pay-per-view audience. How much those viewers pay is based on the main event.

Early fights also help promoters find possible new stars. Undercard matches usually last three or four rounds, or as many as 10 for the fight just before the main event. That high-profile match goes 12 rounds, if it is for a title.

The final fight of the night, in the MGM Grand Garden Arena in Las Vegas, matched Manny Pacquiao against Juan Manuel Márquez. It was the third time they would fight each other. Pacquiao had won the first two, but they were close, each by a split decision. This time, Pacquiao would win again, but by a majority decision. That means that two of the three judges gave the match to Pacquiao, and the third judge rated it as a tie.

The Bradley vs. Casamayor bout right before that

By the time of the Casamayor fight, Tim and Monica had had the first of their three children together.

wasn't exactly overlooked, but its promoter wasn't expecting it to produce much drama.

"We had seen Tim," Bob Arum says. "We knew what a good fighter he was and we thought he would match up well with Manny. Casamayor was a fighter on the downswing, but he had a good name." Arum meant that because Casamayor had been known for a long time, he would sell some tickets. Promoters like to claim that they made the undercard more interesting.

Tim couldn't listen to everybody who was saying he would win easily. He couldn't take anything about Casamayor lightly. If Casamayor seemed old at 40, he also just might have the experience to figure out Tim's speed. If he had one great fight left in him, it might be this one.

All that Tim had dreamed of, and hoped for, was at stake. All those 5 a.m. runs up toward the Palm Springs Aerial Tramway, all the hours in the gym, all the fun he had missed with his friends because he was training, were now put to the test. His goal was to fight Manny Pacquiao, but his mind was on Casamayor.

In boxing, weigh-ins take place the day before the match to ensure the fighters have made weight. That routine used to be held the day of the fight. But sometimes that was dangerous for fighters who were too heavy on the first try, and who struggled the rest of the day to drop enough weight to qualify for the match. By then, sometimes, they were too weak to box well.

In the last 15 years or so, promoters helped to turn weigh-ins into a show of their own. They wanted to boost ticket and pay-per-view sales, so they got reporters and TV broadcasters to watch the fighters enter the weigh-in with their posses. They liked it when fighters talked trash about their opponents, and they had them pose, face-to-face, with a mean glare. They hoped people would think it was dramatic. They hoped to create more excitement for the actual match.

Most of the time, it's just a foolish fake, a circus. But it creates buzz.

Tim and Joel Casamayor had to weigh no more than 140 pounds for their fight. At the Friday weigh-in, Casamayor went first. Following tradition, he stripped down to his underwear and stepped onto the scale. Officials stared at the number. After a long pause, one said, "141 pounds."

The rules gave Casamayor one hour to lose that pound. Welcome to the circus.

First, Casamayor instructed his team to hide his body by holding up shirts in front of him. Then, in the middle of about 20 people onstage, he removed his underwear. No one, not even the buck-naked boxer, really believed his underpants weighed a pound.

"Still 141," the official said.

As Casamayor put his shorts back on, Michael Buffer, a famous ring announcer who was broadcasting the weigh-in, said into his microphone, "Casamayor has an hour. One trip to the bathroom will take care of it."

Tim stepped on the scale: 140. More important,

compared with Casamayor, he looked as buff as Batman. Casamayor headed to the bathroom, talking trash to Tim along the way. Finally an official with Top Rank stepped between them to end the nonsense. But he was grinning.

An hour later, Casamayor had made weight. No one asked how.

The next night, Casamayor had no time to talk trash. He was too busy running and holding. He was too busy looking like he would lose.

Boxing rules say that you may not hold — that is, wrap your arms completely around the opponent — excessively. You may not hit your opponent in the back of the head, which is called a rabbit punch. You may not head-butt on purpose, or throw a punch below the belt. You're not allowed to throw a punch while the referee is separating fighters in a "clinch." You may not hit a fighter after a knockdown, even if he's still on one knee.

A referee may deduct a point if a boxer breaks any of those rules, and even one point can be crucial. When a fighter wins a round, he's awarded 10 points. If he loses a round, he gets nine points from the judge, but the losing fighter gets only eight if a penalty has been called. (A fighter who is knocked down during a round automatically gets eight points for the round.)

Against Tim, Casamayor not only had lots of point deductions, he was clearly outmatched. Tim was quicker, more powerful, and, simply, the better boxer.

Casamayor didn't have fun that night, but the TV announcing team did.

One announcer, noting that both boxers had lost points in other fights for head-butting, joked, "The line going around is that the best butt wins the fight."

Another announcer called Bradley "Tim Lunch Pail." That referred to his hard-work style. It meant he wasn't flashy, and to Tim, it was a compliment.

Tim won every round. It wasn't even close. At the end of the fourth round, Casamayor had landed only four power punches.

Boxing separates fight statistics into jabs and power punches. The power punches are considered to tell more about who is winning than jabs.

By the sixth round, Casamayor had lost one point for holding and Tim had knocked him down twice. Right before the bell to end the sixth, Tim knocked Casamayor down again with a body punch. It was too much, and Casamayor's team stopped the fight.

Tim had posted one of the biggest routs in boxing history. His score would have been 60 points for the first six rounds. Casamayor would have had 18 points for the first two rounds and 50 for the whole fight. In boxing, a 60-50 victory is rarely seen.

Because Pacquiao would beat Márquez in the main event that night, the stage was set for a Bradley vs. Pacquiao match six months later. It would be for the WBO Welterweight title, 147 pounds.

Arum, who promoted both fighters, was happy. As he said, "Bradley killed Casamayor," so a lot of boxing fans would be eager to see a good fight between his two boxers, even though Pacquiao had such a long winning streak.

Arum also was happy dealing with the Bradleys. Somebody asked him if he thought they were good people.

"No, not good," he says. "Excellent. They are tremendous people. They understand what it is all about. I can't say enough good about them."

Everything seemed to be good with the Bradleys. Tim and Monica were married, and Robert and Alaysia Smoot had their first little sister, Jada Bradley, who was born in 2011.

Arum said he thought that Tim would give Pacquiao a good fight. He said that their boxing styles would attract lots of fans and would do well on pay-per-view. Eventually, he would let slip that for fighting Manny Pacquiao on June 9, 2012, Tim's purse would be $5 million. Win or lose.

Of course, everybody just assumed the "lose" part.

9

DID YOU REALLY WIN THE FIGHT?

THE BOXING MATCH between Manny Pacquiao and Tim Bradley was considered among the most important events of a weekend that had a lot to offer sports fans.

At the top of the list was the Belmont. That horse race was especially important in 2012 because a horse named I'll Have Another had a chance to win the Triple Crown. That series of races begins with the Kentucky Derby, moves to the Preakness, and ends with the Belmont. No horse had won all three since 1978.

Even people who didn't like sports, who didn't follow horse racing, would be watching that race because I'll Have Another might win a Triple Crown.

The Belmont would run on Saturday afternoon be-

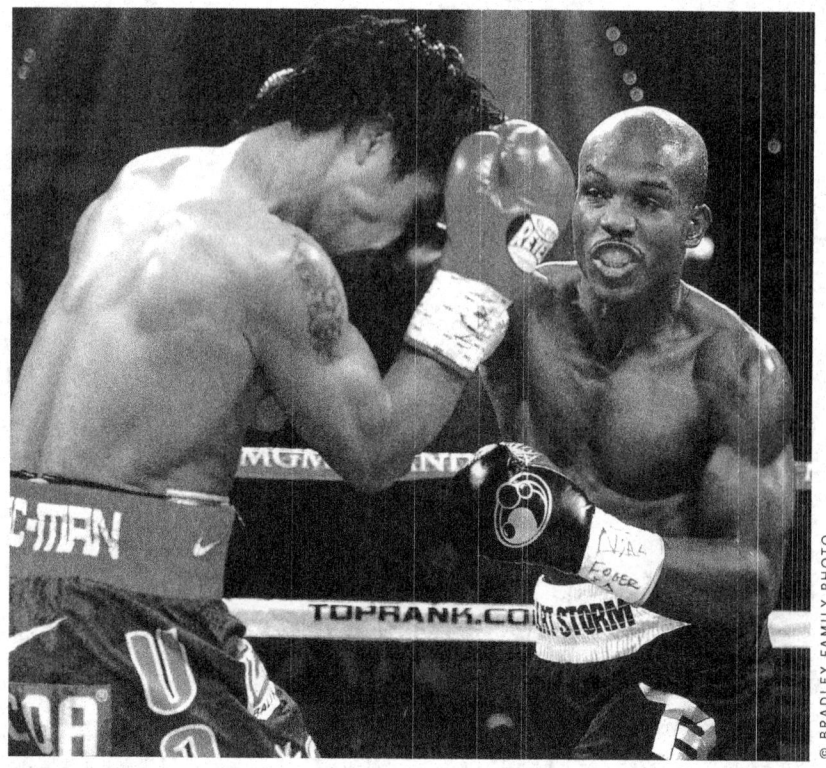

Tim surprised the world in 2012 with his victory over Manny Pacquiao for the WBO Welterweight title.

fore the night Tim would fight the biggest bout of his life.

Tim's story got even bigger that Friday when race officials announced that I'll Have Another had injured his leg and would not run the next day in the Belmont. Sports fans could still watch baseball and basketball and hockey playoffs, but the Pacquiao vs. Bradley fight now loomed even larger.

A championship fight in a big Las Vegas casino is always big news when it includes Manny Pacquiao. The little lefty was born poor in the Philippines, one of six children in the family. When he was 14, he figured that there were too many mouths to feed, so he left home. He became a street kid, hustling fights that, if he won, would pay for food for his family.

Pacquiao was discovered by Bob Arum, who was amazed that this puny kid just kept winning. He wanted him for Top Rank. By the time Arum was promoting his fight with Tim, Pacquiao had won 15 straight professional matches and had not lost in seven years. In addition, in 2010, Pacquiao had been elected to the Philippine Congress.

Pacquiao's story overwhelmed even the tough fighters he met in the ring. So did his left hook.

The fight against Tim was expected to be no different. Tim was just another in a long line of prizefighters who were getting their shot. The fight was at the MGM Grand Garden Arena in Las Vegas, where most of the casinos set odds of Pacquiao winning at 6-1. Those numbers mean that most gamblers believed Pacquiao was six times more likely to win the fight than Tim.

Fight week at the MGM always brings a buzz. The arena would seat about 16,000 people, and about 900,000 more would buy the fight on pay-per-view home viewing. Those TV sales would generate about $50 million. Tim would get a percentage of that, in addition to his $5 million purse.

In interviews during the week before the fight, Tim was respectful of Pacquiao, yet confident. Pacquiao had been through this media circus many times, and he was a master at it. He was also respectful, and confident. Neither fighter was interested in talking trash. Neither one was like that in real life, and knew they didn't need to do it to drum up interest in their bout.

The match started late, well after 9 o'clock in the West. Pacquiao had trouble getting his legs loose, so he stayed in the locker room, riding a stationary bike. When it was time for the fighters to march out, Pacquiao didn't even have his gloves on. That process — wrapping his hands, lacing his gloves — takes at least 15 minutes.

Once the bell rang, Pacquiao started fast, connecting with a lot of punches that made the TV commentators talk as if Tim had no chance. They blamed the seven pounds Tim had gained from his usual weight in order to fight at 147 for Pacquiao's welterweight title. Tim was landing punches, but Pacquiao was landing more.

Freddie Roach, Pacquiao's famous trainer, said he had expected Manny to win all 12 rounds. The unofficial scoring by the TV crew seemed to show that was happening. In this case, "scoring" isn't about who wins a round, it's about how many punches a fighter lands, and about how well he avoids getting hit. So the fighters' scores for all 12 rounds would be in the hundreds — for example, 115-113.

Scoring a boxing match is difficult. You can't always tell if a punch hits the opponent, or just misses. Sometimes, if you think one fighter is going to win, or you like one fighter more than the other, you watch him more. You might miss some of the punches the other guy lands. Everybody assumed that Pacquiao would win. So most people were watching his punches more closely than Tim's.

And Pacquiao was winning. But not by as much as the commentators made it seem.

The only people whose scorecards mattered were the judges — Jerry Roth, Duane Ford, and C.J. Ross. They sat ringside, and scrutinized every move, every hit, every miss.

About the sixth round, the TV commentators were speculating on how long Tim would last. A few rounds later, they sounded amazed that not only was he still on his feet, but he was still throwing punches as hard as the ones he was taking. Nobody had noticed, but early in the fight, Tim had turned over his right ankle, tearing some ligaments. That would have been a good reason to quit. Tim didn't.

Maybe he was still hearing his dad's voice saying, "Never show that you are hurt when you are in the ring."

Later in the fight, the commentators started to sound different. Amazed at how Tim kept fighting, one said, "I don't think anything can stop Tim Bradley's willpower." Another said, equally amazed, "Bradley is still trying to win."

In Tim's corner, his trainer, Joel Diaz, kept telling him, "You are a warrior." Tim's dad, Ray, held an ice pack to the back of his son's head.

When the bell rang to end the last round, both fighters threw their hands in the air, as if they knew they had won. Pacquiao assumed victory because he always won. Tim, dead tired, wasn't sure.

Arum, who promoted both of them, jumped into the ring while the scores were being tabulated. He went over to Tim, whom he quoted later as saying, "I tried as hard as I could, but I just couldn't beat him."

The drama ended with ring announcer Michael Buffer:

"Judge Jerry Roth scores it 115-113, Manny Pacquiao."

Eyes rolled. How could anybody score it that close? A very noisy arena went quiet.

"Judge C.J. Ross scores it 115-113, Tim Bradley."

Say *what?* Reporters typing their stories in press row stopped cold.

"Judge Duane Ford scores it, 115-113 ... FOR THE NEW WBO WELTERWEIGHT CHAMPION ..." Tim Bradley's name was lost in the uproar of boos and screams. The word "new" was all anybody needed to hear.

Surprise turned to shock. A lot of people were angry. Most of the newspaper reporters on a tight deadline had been ready to file their stories about Pacquiao's victory. Now, they leaned back in their chairs in stunned panic. Then they lurched forward, and desperately started typing a story with a new ending, even if they still couldn't believe it.

"My first reaction was to grab Buffer and tell him he had read the scoring wrong, that he needed to get back on the microphone," says Arum, who later called the decision "outlandish."

One announcer, in disbelief, told the cold truth: "Tim Bradley has just scored an upset victory over Manny Pacquiao, and only God knows how." A bit later, he said, it was "a terrible, bogus decision."

The exhausted boxers had more poise than all 16,000 people in the arena. Interviewed in the ring, Tim said he thought it had been a very close fight and that he would "go home and look at the tapes to see if I won." Pacquiao said, "I respect the judges. I do my best, but that wasn't good enough." He was asked if he thought he had won. "Absolutely," he replied.

Still in the ring, Pacquiao turned to Ray Bradley, shook his hand and said, "Your son will make a fine champion."

They held a news conference about 35 minutes later, in a big ballroom at the MGM Grand Hotel. Tim arrived in a wheelchair. His ankle was so badly injured that he couldn't step on it.

One question would haunt Tim for several years.

"Do you really think you won the fight?"

10
THE DARK DAYS

IF TIM THOUGHT he could enjoy his victory over Manny Pacquiao, he was wrong. His greatest moment inflicted his deepest wound. Years later, one sportswriter remembered what it was like in the months after that stunning event:

"Tim Bradley was like a lottery winner who collected his payoff, stepped outside, and was hit by a bus. He was like the bridegroom who was left on the steps of the church while his wife-to-be drove off with her old boyfriend. He was the guy who made a hole-in-one at a golf tournament on the hole where they weren't giving away a car."

For Tim, even that would have been a rosy picture. Right after the fight, Bob Arum of Top Rank Boxing, called for an investigation.

A poll of the 55 reporters scoring the match at ringside showed that 52 had Pacquiao winning. A bigger media survey reported that 121 people had Pacquiao winning, and only three were for Tim.

Even the scorecard of Cameron Dunkin, Tim's manager, had Pacquiao winning, eight rounds to four, or 116-112 — 80 points for the rounds he won, and 36 for the rounds he lost.

A few weeks later, a panel of experienced boxing judges looked at a recording of the fight. All six had Pacquiao winning.

Teddy Atlas, a well-respected commentator for ESPN, called the decision "either corruption or incompetence." No one knew then that a few years later Atlas would become Tim's trainer for another fight with … Manny Pacquiao.

C.J. Ross was one of the two judges who gave the win to Tim that night. By then, she had worked more than 100 title fights, but after that bout, she retired, and never judged another fight. To this day, she has said almost nothing publicly about that night.

Duane Ford, the other judge who ruled that Tim had won, also retired from judging. He had worked more than 200 title fights. He remained a boxing official, and unlike Ross, he expressed a few opinions about the fight.

At first, he said, "Bradley gave Pacquiao a boxing lesson."

Later, he regretted putting it like that. But in an interview with Fox Sports, Ford said, "This isn't 'American Idol.' If I judge for the people, I shouldn't be a judge. I went in with a clean mind and judged each round. I don't look at punch stats. I saw Manny miss a lot of punches and Bradley hit Manny and win a lot of exchanges. I never saw Pacquiao miss so much. HBO said those punches landed. They didn't."

Maybe that was the best clue to the whole mess. Tim's speed often made the other guy miss. That's called defense, and it earns points in boxing matches — when the judges see it. Sometimes, a missed punch is difficult for a fan to spot. But Ross and Ford were not fans. They weren't sitting 30 yards away. They weren't watching on TV. They were right next to the ring.

On top of everything else, most fans saw the controversy as something to prevent what most of them had wanted for a long time: a fight between Pacquiao and Floyd Mayweather Jr. Known for his love of money and flashy lifestyle, Mayweather lives in Las Vegas. Billboards in that city present him and the people who built his career as "The Money Team."

Three years later, in 2015, fans did get to see Pacquiao and Mayweather fight, but by then, neither boxer was in peak condition. It was still a huge deal, but people were still talking about what might have been if Pacquiao had beaten Tim in 2012.

That lost chance was probably why Arum, whose Top Rank company promoted both Pacquiao and Bradley, was so angry with the decision. It made his negotiations with the difficult Mayweather 10 times harder.

Most boxers would have enjoyed being the center of attention for so long. Most boxers would not have cared what people thought or said. Tim Bradley was not most boxers.

Two years later, he told the Daily Mail, a newspaper in England, "It was the darkest period of my life."

How dark? This dark: Tim was getting death threats.

Fred Sternburg, an executive for Top Rank, says, "Tim went through hell. We heard what was going on, about the death threats and cranks calls."

Tim told the Daily Mail that he would sit in bed at night with Monica and think about all that was coming at him.

"Not only did I not want to box again," he said. "I didn't want to live anymore."

He says he couldn't stop wondering what he could have done differently. "I came to the fight, I did my job," he says. "It was a close fight that could have gone either way."

Tim says he sometimes felt guilty, felt like a loser that

he had won. That feeling was different from when he and Monica were nearly out of money, he says. It was different from the fear of not being good enough.

"I was a mess," he says.

It took a long time for Tim to heal. He told the Daily Mail that Monica got him through it. "My wife is great, just terrific, so intelligent. She helped me. Protected my back. Who better to look after me?"

He finally realized that he would have to learn to ignore the mean remarks. He would need a sense of humor. "When I was able to laugh about it," he says, "I came back to the ring."

Tim remembers the day a woman told him that she was one of his biggest fans. She asked about his plans for his next fight. He told her he was fighting Manny Pacquiao again. She said, "Great. I hope you win this time."

Finally, he could laugh.

11

THEY WANT BLOOD

SLOWLY, OVER MOST of the next year, the hurt from the Pacquiao fight eased. Tim was a boxer, and boxers box. It was time.

He said yes to a welterweight title defense bout against Russian boxer Ruslan Provodnikov in 2013, not quite a year after the Pacquiao fight. People wondered about his common sense. As a guy from Palm Springs, Tim was the "Desert Storm"; Provodnikov, from a cold, tough part of Russia, was called "The Siberian Brawler." At least one of those nicknames hinted at what the fight would be like.

Tim's boxing style was about two main things — speed and strategy. He moved around a lot in the ring, and he threw lots of punches at certain times to set up the next series of punches. Provodnikov didn't think about how to move and set up one punch for the next — he just swung away, often wildly and hard. That's what "brawling" is — less of a sport and more of a street fight. Provodnikov expected to take many punches so that he could get close enough to throw a lot of his own.

Provodnikov has another nickname: "Siberian Rocky." That was supposed to remind fans of the old "Rocky" movies, in which the main character is a boxer named Rocky Balboa whose fights were always brutal and bloody.

What was Tim thinking?

The TV commentator answered that question early in the fight.

"Tim Bradley came out in the first round like somebody with something to prove," he said.

For most of Tim's career, people said that he wasn't a big puncher. He was so skilled at the sweet science of boxing that his fights sometimes seemed boring. The other guy couldn't hit him. He was too quick, too smart. But boxing fans want action. They want knockdowns. They want blood.

Tim's prizefighting record was 28-0. He was the welterweight champion of the world. He had won a fight against a boxing legend, Manny Pacquiao. And he was getting little respect.

Tim was especially disappointed when Pacquiao insulted him by rejecting a rematch. "What's to be gained by that?" Pacquiao told the media. "It would just be another one-sided fight."

All of this was weighing on Tim's mind the night of the fight with Provodnikov. The match was outdoors, at the StubHub Center near Los Angeles.

It was the most difficult fight ever for the family of Tim and Monica Bradley.

Not even 20 seconds into the first round Tim was brawling with Provodnikov. Instead of his usual dancing and jabbing, Tim was leaning into the Russian and swinging wildly. He was fighting Provodnikov's fight, not his.

Provodnikov was better at it. Soon, Tim was in trouble. In the first two rounds, he seemed to be struggling to stay upright. Once, he fell to the canvas, but the referee ruled that it was a slip, not a knockdown. That ruling saved Tim the loss of a point in the scoring.

After the first two rounds, one broadcaster gave Tim what boxing fans would call a compliment: "Most fighters who are alive today would have been knocked out by now."

Tim was earning the respect he wanted, but at a terrible price.

By the third round, two ringside seats were empty.

Tim's fight against Ruslan Provodnikov in 2013 was more of a brawl than a bout.

Monica and Kathleen, his mom, had walked out. The beating Tim was taking was too painful to watch.

Monica, who was pregnant at the time, says, "I had seen enough."

So had Kathleen, who says, "I just couldn't take it."

As always, Ray was in Tim's corner, helping with instructions and medical aid between rounds. But this was a fight like never before.

"It took the life right out of me," Ray says. "At one point, I was scrambling to get up to the corner and I tripped on a cameraman. I went down, flat. The fight had made me so weak, I wanted to just lie there. It was

During training or a prizefight, Ray was always in his son's corner between rounds, giving him ice or water.

like I had been taking all the punishment Tim had.

"But something told me, 'You got to get up. Your son needs you. He is a warrior, and you have to be a warrior, too.'"

Robert Smoot — Tim's stepson and Monica's oldest child — summed up the family's feelings.

"I like it when he boxes," Robert says. "I don't like it when he brawls."

Finally, Tim changed his strategy. His trainer, Joel Diaz, yelled at him until he got through. Instead of brawling, Tim started jabbing, dancing, counterpunching. After losing the first two rounds, Tim won six of the next seven. He did it with basic boxing skills that were scoring points.

Provodnikov was exhausted. His left eye was cut and bleeding. The referee checked with each corner between rounds to see if either fighter was ready to stop. Both trainers considered it.

Words of high praise for Tim flowed from the TV announcers.

"Courageous."

"Spectacular willpower."

"The very definition of a champion."

"What a war!"

Provodnikov's trainer, Freddie Roach, came close to not allowing his fighter to go back out for the 12th and final round. But he did, telling Provodnikov that his only chance to win was to knock out Tim Bradley.

He nearly did. He hit Tim once, then twice, with huge punches. Tim was badly hurt. His legs were like rubber. All he could do was duck and weave and hold on.

Then, he used his best tool — his intelligence.

With 12 seconds left in the fight, and with Provodnikov closing for one last, big punch, Tim dropped to one knee. He knew that would be scored as a knockdown, and that it would cost him a point for the last round. But he was pretty sure he was far enough ahead on the judges' scorecards for the other rounds that one point wouldn't matter.

The rules say that if a fighter is on one knee his opponent may not hit him, so Provodnikov lost his shot. Tim knew that all he had to do was to stand up a second or two before the referee counted to 10, and the clock would run out. The bell would ring, the fight would be over and, he would win.

And he did. Provodnikov had landed the hardest punches, but Tim had won more points. All three judges agreed.

The bout was so brutal and interesting that a boxing writers group voted Bradley vs. Provodnikov as Fight of the Year for 2013. Tim had won thousands of new fans, especially the bloodthirsty kind. People involved in the sport of boxing called the fight a huge success.

Monica Bradley called it a disaster.

In the ring after the fight, Tim said he was sure he had suffered a concussion. That's a brain injury you can have after a blow to the head. Asked how he knew he had a concussion, Tim said, "Because I was dizzy. I'm dizzy right now."

Tim Bradley was a dizzy, unbeaten pro boxer. His record was 30-0. He was in his prime, a world champion sports star earning millions of dollars. He was 29 years old, and his dream had come true.

His joy was not fully shared by Monica. She worried about what Tim would be like when he was 50 or 60 years old. She knew the stories about great boxers who got fame and money, but also brain damage. Monica loved Tim — not his fame, but his heart, and his brain.

After most of the body pain and the headaches from the fight went away, Monica took Tim to the East Coast, to some of the top concussion-care hospitals in the country. There would be no more boxing matches unless Tim got a clean bill of health.

At least that's what Monica hoped.

12
HIS KIND OF FIGHT

FOR YEARS, sports concussions were taken lightly. Sometimes, they were almost like a badge of honor — if you hadn't had at least one concussion, you weren't a "real" athlete.

Today, we know the danger even one such brain injury can pose. And it didn't matter to Monica that her husband was a real athlete. Her fear was the long-term problems he might have from being hit so hard in the head so often.

The real push to study concussions started in the National Football League. Monica was familiar with the dangers of that game. Robert was in middle school by now, and was determined to play high school football. She knew that more and more retired NFL players were reporting problems as they got older. They had bad headaches, and they couldn't remember things most people do. Some were no longer able to speak, or walk. More than other groups, ex-NFL players suffered from lots of illnesses often caused by brain damage.

One night Robert was practicing with his football team and Tim was helping to coach. Monica watched from the bleachers as her son made a hard tackle. She shrugged and said, "This is my life. I have a son and a husband who like to hit people."

Ex-NFL players with brain problems and their families sued the NFL. They went to court to try to get the NFL to pay for the damage they said the league should have known could occur from playing football. They said the NFL should have warned them about this possible cost of playing the game.

But boxers always knew.

Tim talks with amazement about the tests they did on his brain during his trip East with Monica after the Provodnikov fight.

They took pictures of his brain. "You could see all the colors of my brain," he says, "how the sections connected, where the damage was. I could see it all. Where the damage was, where there were blocks."

It was scary.

"After that," Tim says, "I knew where I stood. ... I

For the second time in 2013, Tim defended his WBO Welterweight title. The fight, against Juan Manual Márquez, brought Tim's record to 31-0.

could see the damage that had been done from being hit in fights.

"Physically, I could still fight. There was nothing wrong there. I could still move, still snap my jab. But my brain was totally different from when I was 23."

But, he says, "The doctors never said that I couldn't keep fighting. They just said that, if I continue to fight, this [brain damage] will worsen. So, I'm all right, I'm sharp. But I know I can't make the mistake of staying too long."

Tim wasn't even 30 years old. He had been in 31 professional fights, and had won all but one. That one ended without a decision for either boxer, which boxing calls a "no-contest." Tim had beaten one of the sport's biggest stars, Manny Pacquiao. He and Monica would never have to worry about having only $11. It seemed like a good time to retire from boxing.

But athletes seldom are able to see the bottom when they are at the top.

Tim was living at the top.

"The hardest part," he says, "is that you still have that fire. ... You are torn. There is all kinds of stuff going on in your life, away from boxing, that is great. Your kids are good. You have money. There is really no reason to go on.

"But ... you watch boxing on TV. You see guys you can beat. You don't want them talking about Pacquiao without mentioning your name. You should be in that conversation. I've done that. I've done more.

"Pretty soon, it gets to the point where that's what it is about. It's not about money. It's that you still have it, you can still do it. You want a shot."

Seven months later, Tim took a shot. On Oct. 12, 2013, at the Thomas & Mack Center in Las Vegas, he fought Juan Manuel Márquez.

Once again, it was more than just another boxing match. Six months after Tim got the controversial win over Pacquiao, the Philippine star was knocked out by Márquez. It was a stunning sight — Pacquiao had stayed down, flat on his face, for more than a minute. It was the fourth time he and Márquez had fought, and Pacquiao had won the first three. But every fight had been close, and every decision had been controversial.

Now, if Tim beat Márquez, people who thought his win over Pacquiao was fake might think again. Márquez was 40 years old, 10 years older than Tim. But his amazing knockout of Pacquiao made people forget that.

What they will remember from that October night in Las Vegas is that Tim won. Two of the three judges gave the decision to Tim in a close, but clear, fight.

More important, Tim stayed with his usual style. He fought his kind of fight, moving and jabbing and keeping away from Márquez. He punched fast and moved back faster. The judges, and most of the fans, saw and understood this.

"Márquez is a great counter-puncher," Tim says. "I stayed away so I wouldn't get caught like Manny did. We had a good plan for the fight."

A counter-puncher tries to score off the other fighter's attack. He lets the other boxer start the punching. Many counter-punchers know they will take a few punches just to get a chance to throw their own. Márquez knocked out Pacquiao when Pacquiao attacked, and missed. That threw him off balance when

Márquez punched him in the jaw.

Tim says he figured out how to fight Márquez partly by watching how he had fought, and lost, to Floyd Mayweather Jr. "He has to be set to punch," Tim says. "He won't abandon balance for offense. Everything has to be perfectly correct for him."

Like many boxers who lose, Márquez disagreed with the judges after his fight with Tim.

"I am more scared of the judges in Las Vegas," he said, "than I am of my opponents."

Márquez wasn't the only one on his team who had something to say after the fight. His trainer, Nacho Beristain, told the Guardian, an English newspaper, "Tim Bradley is a very good fighter. He is also a very lucky one. He is the only undefeated boxer I know with two losses."

No matter what, it seemed, the thing Tim might always be remembered for was his controversial win over Pacquiao.

But now, controversy didn't bother him. The Márquez fight was the fifth bout in a row for which his purse was more than $1 million. His record was 31-0. He was just 30 years old, and he was the WBO Welterweight Champion of the world.

And the way he beat Márquez had made his family happy. They weren't talking about concussions. They were talking about his next opponent. His name was familiar.

13
THE FIGHT TO RIGHT A WRONG

TIM BRADLEY and Manny Pacquiao would end up fighting a trilogy. That means two fighters are so competitive and appealing to fans that their promoters can keep selling fights between them. A trilogy is three fights with the same two guys.

Even though Pacquiao at first had said no to a rematch with Tim, it was likely to happen. Tim's brawling win over Provodnikov and his big, strategic win over Márquez kept him high on the list of boxers waiting to fight Pacquiao for the huge payday it promised.

The stage was set. Pacquiao vs. Bradley II would be April 12, 2014 at the MGM Grand Garden Arena in Las Vegas. Tim's purse would be $6 million, and he would get more from the pay-per-view revenue. Pacquiao would get $20 million, plus pay-per-view money. Tim had won the first fight, but he understood why Pacquiao's purse was so much bigger — Manny Pacquiao was a legend. People all over the world knew who he was. Tim was just starting to be famous outside of the boxing community. In boxing, being popular is as important as winning.

Tim's team knew he was in for a tough fight. Pacquiao was 35, but he didn't seem to have lost much. He seemed to have gotten over the knockout by Márquez, and he had fought so often in Las Vegas that it was like his home arena now. This time, a close fight would mean victory for Pacquiao.

Tim's trainer, Joel Diaz, said it best. "We can't just move around and leave it to the judges," he said. "We know that."

In their first fight, remember, Tim had injured his ankle. At the time, Tim had told the media that he had made a mistake — in addition to hurting his ankle, he hadn't worn socks and his feet got very sore.

Pacquiao's famous trainer, Freddie Roach, was still at the top of his game as the mostly quiet trash-talker who didn't always need words: In the weeks before Pacquiao vs. Bradley II, Roach sent a big box of socks to the Bradley training camp.

This is how people with class talk trash.

The fight promotion generated lots of nicknames. One was the "Fight to Right a Wrong." Tim knew that if he were overpowering this time, nobody would question it if he were judged the winner.

But that would be very hard against Pacquiao, who can throw as many as 1,000 punches in a bout. And if a lot of them missed, it was hard to tell. Of course, the victory would be clear if Tim knocked out Pacquiao. But in 62 fights, that had happened only twice to Pacquiao.

And it wouldn't happen this time.

Pacquiao won the fight. All three judges thought he had won, two with a score of 116-112, or eight rounds to four, the third by 118-110, or 10 rounds to two. Even though it ended as everyone expected, it was a great fight that generated a lot more respect for Tim Bradley.

After they announced the decision, Tim stood in his corner and clapped for Pacquiao. He told promoter Bob Arum, "I tried. I really tried. I knew I had to do more than last time."

In the ring, Tim told the TV broadcasters, "You can't say anything bad about Manny. ... He's the toughest in the world, an eight-division world champion. I lost to one of the best in the world, man."

This is how people with class lose.

In 2014, Tim lost the second of his three fights against Manny Pacquiao. It was his first defeat as a prizefighter. Two years later, he would lose again to the great Filipino boxer. They were the only fights he ever lost as a professional.

Tim, who had been fighting since second grade, finally had lost his first professional fight. Now, his record was 31-1. As a kid, he had lost only a few amateur bouts.

For some people, their first loss is devastating. Not for Tim Bradley. He was fond of saying, "I'm a C-level celebrity. I know that and I'm fine with it. I can take my kids to Disneyland, walk around there all day and nobody will bother me. Manny can't do that."

To complete their trilogy, Tim and Pacquiao fought again two years later, on April 9, 2016.

But before that, Tim fought three times. He beat Brandon Rios and Jesse Vargas, and he had a draw — or tie — against Diego Chavez.

Pacquiao fought twice during that time, including once against Floyd Mayweather Jr. All three judges said he had lost to Mayweather in the fight fans had wanted for years. Millions of people purchased the pay-per-view broadcast, making it the richest boxing match of all time. But Pacquiao vs. Mayweather turned out to be a huge disappointment. The score was a rout for Mayweather, and after it was over, Pacquiao reported that he had hurt his shoulder in the fourth round. He said he had no power in that hand for the rest of the fight.

Boxing fans were angry, they felt cheated. Right away, the popularity of boxing seemed to dip.

People still felt that way for Pacquiao vs. Bradley III. Bob Arum still promoted both fighters, and he knew boxing fans were upset over Mayweather vs. Pacquiao. He knew Pacquiao had lost some of his fame, and he knew this fight was a gamble.

But true boxing fans still wanted to see it.

One reason was that it was the third match in a series that was tied, 1-1. That kind of tiebreaker is called a rubber match.

True fans also knew that Tim had a new trainer. Monica had taken over as his manager for the second Pacquiao fight and she would manage this one, too. Now, Tim was trained by Teddy Atlas, who once trained Mike Tyson, the heavyweight champion. And, as a famous boxing commentator on ESPN, he had dissed the decision after Tim's first fight with Pacquiao.

Ray Bradley was thrilled with the change.

"Even before Tim started to fight," Ray said, "I used to watch boxing on TV all the time. I learned everything I know about the sport by listening to Teddy Atlas."

Tim was excited, too. "My kids loved him, my wife loved him," he says of Atlas. "And I can't even describe how much he taught me. By the time I got to the fight, I wasn't as afraid of Manny as I was of screwing up for Teddy."

Freddie Roach was still in Pacquiao's corner, and still smart and mouthy. Somebody asked him what he thought of Atlas's ability as a trainer. He ducked. He weaved. He landed a classy punch, saying, "He's a great broadcaster, a great storyteller."

About a month before the fight, Pacquiao made some disturbing statements about gays and lesbians. His words were mean and hurtful, and they made headlines all over the world. Arum is a well-known supporter of human rights and freedom for all people. He disagreed with Pacquiao, but his job was to promote his fighter.

He said he didn't like Pacquiao's ideas, but that he supported his right to free speech.

Pacquiao's comments also put Tim in a tough spot. Pacquiao's words might affect ticket sales or pay-per-view buys for the fight, and Tim didn't want to say the wrong thing. He also didn't want to anger Pacquiao. It was hard enough to fight against him without giving him more reasons to fight back harder. In the end, Tim just said what he felt.

"I respect people for what they are," he said. "I judge people by their heart."

The issue faded fast. Pacquiao didn't duck questions about it, but he was training in the Philippines. By the time he arrived in the United States for the bout, the biggest pre-fight story was that Pacquiao had announced that this would be his last fight.

But boxers are always retiring, then un-retiring. The bright lights of fame and the big paychecks are hard to give up. Still, Pacquiao's announcement seemed like it might be true. He was deep into Philippine politics, and he wanted to be elected to that country's Senate. He already was a congressman in his country's House of Representatives, but there are 297 of them. There are only 24 senators.

"I fought because I wanted to help my family," he said. "Now I will stop, because I want to help my country."

Except for Roach's funny insult about Teddy Atlas, the fight promotion was mostly friendly. "There is no villain here," Roach said. By now, Tim and Pacquiao knew each other well. They liked each other. Tim even told reporters that Pacquiao was a good person and should be elected to the Senate.

In the ring, Pacquiao made it clear that he wanted to retire in glory. He was on Tim from the opening bell and knocked him down twice. Tim wasn't hurt badly, and he clearly was a better boxer than he was in the first two fights. But even at 37 years old, Pacquiao was better.

"He's a special fighter," Tim says now. "His punches are heavy. They hurt. He moves differently than any other boxer. He is on you and then he is gone. Speed and power. When he punches, it is deadly."

All three judges scored the fight 116-112 for Pacquiao, eight rounds to four. It was a good match, but the pay-per-view sales were only a little more than half of what they were for Pacquiao vs. Bradley II.

Seven months later, Pacquiao un-retired. He had won his Senate seat, and then he won his fight with Jesse Vargas. As Tim had 18 months earlier, Pacquiao beat Vargas solidly — all three judges said so.

14

THE VALUE OF LIFE

WHEN PEOPLE BECOME FAMOUS, they often forget what it was like when they weren't. Not Tim Bradley.

He still talks about the days when he and Monica had only $11. He still remembers driving up to their house only to find an eviction notice on the front door. He still talks about growing up in a neighborhood that turned kids into gang members.

"I saw so many great athletes in my neighborhood," he says. "I'd go to the recreation center and there were guys playing basketball. They were good. Really good. One of them was 6-foot-11.

"I think I'm the only one who got out."

Today, in 2017, he has five boxing world championships. He has five children. He's prouder of the people than the trophies.

When Tim was a kid, his parents had rules. Now that he has kids of his own, he and Monica also have rules.

One: Work comes before fun. The children know that before they go out to play, they must finish their homework.

Two: Doing less than your best work in school won't cut it.

A couple of years ago, Robert Smoot, Tim's stepson, was not working as hard in one class as his mother wanted. He passed, but Monica made him take the class over anyway. He passed again, but this time his grade was much higher. "You can't get into college with C's," Monica told her son.

Three: Be kind to other people.

Tim is concerned that kids today spend so much time on Facebook, on their phones, playing video games, that they don't see the world as it really is instead of how it looks on a screen. "They don't see things around them," he says. "All they see is what is on their phones.

"I get upset when my kids don't say 'Thank you.' I walk down the street and … pass 15 people. I say hello to all of them. It doesn't matter whether they answer back. I just want to say it. Everything in the world these days seems to be me, me, me, me. We don't want our kids to be that way."

One day in early 2017, the family was shopping in downtown Palm Springs. It was a rare cold, rainy day. They passed an old woman, crouched under the overhang of a large store for protection against the rain. She had no hat, no coat. She was shivering.

The Bradleys went inside the store where the kids bought candy. Tim and Monica picked up some other items. As they paid at the checkout, the children saw things they hadn't expected their parents to buy — a coat, some gloves, some food. When they got outside, Tim asked the children to give these things to the woman who had nothing.

"She cried," Tim says. He wanted his family to see what he saw, that "others aren't always as fortunate as you are. That's the value of life I want to show my kids."

There are a lot of wealthy people in the Coachella Valley where the Bradleys live. But there are a lot of poor people, too, and many groups that try to help them. The Bradleys give money to some of those groups, including one set up by his boxing trainer, Teddy Atlas. Tim says the Atlas Foundation helps "whomever and whatever needs help. If it is surgery, they pay for it. If it is a bed, a car, they will look at it and help out."

15

THE LONG RIDE HOME

BY OCTOBER 2017, it had been a year and a half since Tim Bradley stepped into the ring against a professional fighter. That doesn't mean he relaxed. He spent a lot of time at his training gym in the Coachella Valley helping younger boxers learn the sport he was so lucky to have learned when he was young.

He also began a career as a boxing commentator. On July 2, 2017, he went to Australia as part of ESPN's broadcast team for the title fight between Manny Pacquiao and Jeff Horn.

That bout turned out to be as shocking as Tim's first fight with Pacquiao. Horn was expected to lose, maybe even by a knockout early in the fight. But the match went 12 rounds. By all accounts, viewers and broadcasters thought Pacquiao had won. Tim was the only announcer who said it was closer than most people thought.

The judges did too. They gave the fight to Horn.

That was a huge turning point in the career of Jeff Horn. And for Tim Bradley.

On the plane home from Australia the next day, Tim retired from boxing. While Monica slept, Tim walked to where Teddy Atlas was sitting. Atlas had been part of the broadcast with Tim, and had become like a second father to him.

When he was in college, Tim helped a young fighter learn the sport. Now retired from boxing, Tim still helps youngsters the way O.J. Couture helped him when he was 10.

"He asked me why I wanted to continue to fight," Tim says. "I told him that one reason was that I wanted to see if I can still compete on that high level. And part of me wanted to grab some more of that money." Monica was starting a new restaurant business, and Tim wanted to help her grow it.

"Teddy said, 'Stop. Do you still have the desire to be great?' I said I didn't know, but I would know once I stepped into that ring again. He said that would be too late, that we couldn't wait that long."

Tim went back to his seat in the plane. Monica woke up and he told her.

"I had sat there, watching Pac [Pacquiao], and saw the hell he was going through," Tim says. "I asked myself if I wanted to be in there with Horn now. The old Tim Bradley would have said I'd mop the floor with Horn. This day-and-age Tim Bradley ... didn't want to be in there anymore."

Tim says much of his decision was about his kids. He says he spent much of the summer with them at a home they have in San Diego while Monica worked on her new restaurant project in Rancho Mirage. He says he couldn't have enjoyed it more.

Children of the blended Bradley family relax at home in the desert. From left to right, Malaya Bradley, Alaysia Smoot, Jada Bradley, Robert Smoot, Malakai Bradley.

"I don't have that fire anymore. My fire is my kids. I wanted to retire from boxing. I didn't want boxing to retire me."

Tim's stepson Robert is in his last year of high school football. Robert's sister, Alaysia Smoot, is interested in making films. The children he had with Monica — Jada, Malaya, and the baby Malakai — are showing skills of their own. Jada wasn't even in first grade when she won a reading award in 2017.

Robert is too small to play football in college, but after he graduates, he wants to go to the University of Michigan. Tim knows that such a good school will demand excellent grades.

"He is transitioning from a football player to somebody focusing on his studies," Tim says of Robert. "He is playing football because he wants to be with his friends. He knows the challenges ahead and I think, now, that he really wants it. The Michigan thing is partly because he wants to please me, I think. I'm a big Michigan fan."

Alaysia is a straight-A student. Tim says she is like her mother — a "go-getter."

"If Alaysia is given a project and has two weeks to complete it," Tim says, "she will want to start on it right away."

Jada the reader is the family's little jock. At 5 years old, she was the best hitter on her softball team, even better than the boys. She also likes to play soccer.

"She will score three or four goals in every soccer game she plays," Tim says. "You know those soccer games where the little kids sit down or play in the sand or just stare at the sky? Jada never did that once. She wanted the action. She wanted the game."

Malaya, who goes to pre-school, is very neat. She's also quiet, but she expects a lot from people, and she can be a leader when she needs to step up. Tim says she, too, is like Monica. "You need to prove things to her first."

Malakai, says Tim, is "smart. Maybe too smart for his own good," he adds. "If I take him to the swimming pool, I stay right there," he says, because Malakai is so fast and feisty, he would jump in the water by himself if you let him. "He loves danger," Tim says.

And Monica? The woman who held two jobs, raised two kids, and managed a house when most people her age were going to college or partying with friends? Monica has more energy than anyone else in the family. In addition to her new restaurant — Haus of Poké — she manages a few young fighters whom Tim is training.

So boxing remains part of Tim's life. His first few broadcasting jobs analyzing boxing matches were successful.

Now, Tim punches less and talks more.

AFTERWORD

IN 1991, A SECOND-GRADER got into a lot of trouble. He tried to get out of it using his fists. He wasn't always nice to people.

One day, one of his classmates who was disabled, backed his wheelchair over the kid's foot. He told him to stop it. Instead, he rolled his wheelchair over his foot again. The kid who liked to talk with his fists got angry. He pushed over the wheelchair with the disabled child in it.

Today, the man who was that mean kid covers his face with his hands and groans when he's reminded of that story. His name is Tim Bradley.

"I was such a bad kid," he says.

But he learned to use his anger in a different way, he learned to care about other people who didn't have the gifts he was given.

Not long ago, Tim saw a man in Palm Springs with whom he had gone to high school. He hadn't seen him for years, not since they were teenagers. The man, dressed in rags, was looking into some garbage bins.

Clearly, he was homeless. Tim walked up to him, and reminded him that they knew each other from school.

The man remembered, but he was too ashamed to say much.

It was very hot that day, and Tim's old friend had no shoes. Soon, his feet would burn in the heat.

Tim Bradley, the millionaire world champion professional boxer, took off his shoes and gave them to the man.

TIM BRADLEY TIMELINE

EARLY CHILDHOOD: 1983-1993

AUGUST 1983 – The second of three children is born to Ray and Kathleen. Named Timothy Ray Bradley, he goes by Tim.

1990 – As a second-grader, Tim is angry, gets into trouble, and is expelled from school.

1992 – Tim continues to get into fights and is expelled from another school.

1993 – 10-year-old Tim learns to box at a gym. He loses his first club fight, against his school friend.

LATER SCHOOL YEARS: 1995-2003

1995 – Tim trains regularly with his boxing club. He wins six Junior Olympic titles in six years as he and his family travel many weekends to tournaments.

1996 – Tim discovers girls. His grades go from A's to F's. His parents forbid him from boxing for two months. He performs extra chores, and brings his grades back up. He resumes training.

2001 – Tim graduates from high school. He earns a scholarship to Northern Michigan University, and participates in the Olympic boxing training program. For the first time, he lives in a cold climate.

2003 – Tim does well, but does not make the Olympic team. He does not like the cold weather. He tells his parents he wants to leave school and become a professional boxer.

EARLY PROFESSIONAL BOXING CAREER: 2004-2008

AUGUST 2004 – 20-year-old Tim wins his first pro fight with a knockout of Francisco Martinez in Corona, California.

2005 – By the end of the year, Tim's professional record is 10-0. But his matches are low-level and pay little even though he has won a World Youth title.

2006 – Tim trains, boxes, and works as a server in a restaurant, where he runs into a friend from high school, Monica Manzo. They begin to date.

2008 – Tim and Monica are living together. Even though Tim is undefeated as a boxer (21-0), money is still scarce, and he and Monica both work several jobs.

MARCH 2008 – Tim gets his first big fight. It's in Mexico, against Jose Luis Castillo, a local star. Castillo fails to make weight, and the fight is canceled. Tim and Monica lose a lot of money.

MAY 2008 – Monica and Tim have only $11 in the bank when they travel to England, where Tim fights for a major world championship title against Junior Witter. Tim wins and takes home $52,000.

LATER PROFESSIONAL CAREER: 2008-2017

2008-2011 – Tim wins five more fights. He is now promoted by boxing's best-known company, Top Rank.

2010 – Tim and Monica marry.

2012 – Tim fights boxing's best known and best-loved star, Manny Pacquiao, in Las Vegas, for another world championship. He stuns the world with a controversial win. The victory is unpopular in the boxing world. The negative attention pushes Tim into a deep depression.

2013 – Tim fights Russian Ruslan Provodnikov in a brutal defense of his world title. Tim gets knocked down, suffers a concussion, but still wins. Boxing writers calls it the Fight of the Year. Tim proves to the world that he deserves his high status.

SUMMER 2013 – Monica takes over as Tim's manager. Worried about brain injury from the concussion, Tim and Monica visit famous brain injury doctors. Tim gets a clean bill of health on brain scans, but sees how different his brain looks now, at age 29, from how it looked when he was 23.

APRIL 2014 – Tim fights Pacquiao in a rematch. For the first time in his professional career, he loses. His record is 31-1.

2015 – Monica is nominated by the Boxing Writers Association of America as Manager of the Year.

APRIL 2016 – Tim fights Pacquiao for the last time. He loses.

JULY 2016 – Tim works as an analyst for a high-profile fight on HBO.

2017 – Tim becomes a boxing commentator for ESPN on several high-level matches. He works with his former trainer, Teddy Atlas.

AUGUST 2017 – With a professional record of 33-2-1, Tim retires from boxing.

TIM BRADLEY'S PRO BOXING CAREER
33-2-1

DATE	AGAINST	LOCATION	SCORE	COMMENTS
August 20, 2004	Francisco Martinez	Omega Products International, Corona, CA	Bradley 1-0	Technical Knockout
October 29, 2004	Raul Nunez	Doubletree Hotel, Ontario, CA	2-0	Unanimous Decision
November 22, 2004	Luis Medina	Doubletree Ontario, CA	3-0	Knockout
March 28, 2005	Carlos Perra	Doubletree Ontario, CA	4-0	Knockout
April 25, 2005	Ramon Prtiz	Doubletree Ontario, CA	5-0	Knockout
June 3, 2005	Justo Almazan	Doubletree Ontario, CA	6-0	Unanimous Decision
July 21, 2005	Marcos Andre Roche Costa	Los Angeles Athletic Club	7-0	Technical Knockout
August 26, 2005	Juan Yoani Cervantes	Omega Products International, Corona, CA	8-0	Unanimous Decision
September 23, 2005	Francisco Rincon	Omega Products International, Corona, CA	9-0	Unanimous Decision
November 21, 2005	Jorge Alberto Padilla	Doubletree Ontario, CA	10-0	Technical Decision
February 17, 2006	Rafael Ortiz	Doubletree Ontario, CA	11-0	Referee Technical Decision
March 31, 2006	Eli Addison	Doubletree Ontario, CA	12-0	Unanimous Decision
May 13, 2006	Jesus Abel Santiago	Antelope Valley Fairgrounds Lancaster, CA	13-0	Knockout
June 23, 2006	Arturo Arena	Doubletree Ontario, CA	14-0	Technical Knockout
August 16, 2006	Martin Ramirez	Omega Products International, Corona, CA	15-0	Referee Technical Decision
October 16, 2006	Alfonso Sanchez	Doubletree Ontario, CA	16-0	Knockout
December 1, 2006	Jaime Rangel	Chumash Casino, Santa Ynez, CA	17-0	Technical Decision
February 2, 2007	Manuel Garnica	Chumash Casino, Santa Ynez, CA	18-0	Unanimous Decision

DATE	AGAINST	LOCATION	SCORE	COMMENTS
April 13, 2007	Nassar Nathumani	Doubletree Hotel Ontario, CA	19-0	Technical Knockout
June 1, 2007	Donald Camerena	Chumash Casino, Santa Ynez, CA	20-0	Unanimous Decision
July 27, 2007	Miguel Vasquez	Omega Products International, Corona, CA	21-0	Unanimous Decision
May 10, 2008	Jumior Witter	Nottingham Arena Nottingham, England	22-0	Split Decision For WBC 140-pound Super Light Weight title
September 13, 2008	Ebner Cherry	Beau Rivage Resort Casino, Biloxi, MS	23-0	Unanimous Decision
April 4, 2009	Kendall Holt	Bell Center Montreal, Canada	24-0	Unanimous Decision Won WBO Super Light Weight title
August 1, 2009	Nate Campbell	Agua Caliente Casino Rancho Mirage, CA	24-0	Ruled no contest because of head-butts causing a fight stoppage before the fourth round
December 12, 2009	Lamont Peterson	Agua Caliente Casino Rancho Mirage, CA	25-0	Unanimous Decision
July 17, 2010	Luis Carlos Abregu	Agua Caliente Casino Rancho Mirage, CA	26-0	Unanimous Decision
January 29, 2011	Devon Alexander	Silverdome Pontiac, MI	27-0	Technical Decision
November 12, 2011	Joel Casamayor	MGM Grand Garden Arena Las Vegas, NV	28-0	Technical Knockout
June 9, 2012	Manny Pacquiao	MGM Grand Garden Arena Las Vegas, NV	29-0	Split Decision Won WBO Welterweight title
March 16, 2013	Ruslan Provodnikov	Home Depot Center Carson, CA	30-0	Unanimous Decision
October 12, 2013	Juan Manel Márquez	Thomas & Mack Center Las Vegas, NV	31-0	Split Decision
April 12, 2014	Manny Pacquiao	MGM Grand Garden Arena Las Vegas, NV	31-1	Unanimous Decision Lost WBO Welterweight title
December 13, 2014	Diego Chavez	Cosmopolitan Las Vegas, NV	31-1-1	Draw
June 27, 2015	Jessie Vargas	StubHub Center Carson, CA	32-1-1	Unanimous Decision Won Interim WBO Welterweight title
November 7, 2015	Brandon Rios	Thomas & Mack Center Las Vegas, NV	33-1-1	Technical Knockout Regained WBO Welterweight title
April 9, 2016	Manny Pacquiao	MGM Grand Garden Arena Las Vegas, NV	33-2-1	Unanimous Decision Lost WBO Welterweight title

GLOSSARY OF BOXING TERMS, ORGANIZATIONS, AND NOTABLE PEOPLE

A

AMATEUR—Boxer who competes in tournaments without getting paid.

B

BOB ARUM—Founder and head of Top Rank, one of the major boxing promotion companies.

BODYBUILDER—Person who lifts weights and trains to become muscular for competitions comparing his or her looks against those of other muscular competitors.

BODY PUNCH—Hitting above the belt and below the chin.

BOXING WRITERS ASSOCIATION OF AMERICA—Membership organization of journalists who report on the sport of boxing.

BRAWLING—Swinging freely during a bout instead of strategically setting up punches.

C

CHAMPIONSHIP BELT—Awarded to boxers who win world titles for a sanctioning group. They are oversized, colorful, and covered with jewels.

COMMENTATOR—Broadcaster who analyzes the fight for TV viewers.

CONCUSSION—Mild-to-severe brain injury with temporary or permanent effects usually caused by a blow to the head.

COUNTER-PUNCHER—Boxer whose style or strategy is to let the other fighter strike first, then attack in response.

CUT MAN—Person who treats the fighter's cuts in his corner between rounds during a match.

D

DEMENTIA—Decreased ability to think, speak, and function. Symptoms include memory loss. Caused by brain damage from head trauma or from diseases or disorders such as Alzheimer's or strokes.

DESERT STORM—Nickname of boxer Tim Bradley because he is from the desert and is known for throwing a lot of punches with speed.

F

FLOYD MAYWEATHER JR. —World champion boxer in five different weight divisions, known for superior defense and flashy lifestyle.

FREDDIE ROACH—Hall of Fame boxing trainer best known for handling Manny Pacquiao.

G

GOLDEN GLOVES—National series of amateur boxing tournaments, sponsored by USA Boxing.

H

HAND WRAPS—Cloth covering around the boxer's fists under the gloves.

HEAD-BUTT—Boxer's head hits opponent's head, opening a cut. Usually it's accidental, but if the referee rules it intentional, a penalty can be assessed, or a boxer can be disqualified.

HEADGEAR—Protective covering for boxers' heads when they are sparring.

HEAVY BAG—Equipment in a boxing gym that hangs from the ceiling on a chain and usually weighs between 100 and 150 pounds.

HOOK—Boxing punch thrown with the elbow away from the body.

I

INTERNATIONAL BOXING FEDERATION—IBF, a sanctioning group.

J

JAB—Set-up punch in a boxing match. Right-handers jab with the left hand, left-handers with the right hand.

JOEL CASAMAYOR—Olympic gold medal winning boxer for Cuba who later defected to the U.S.

JUAN MANUEL MÁRQUEZ—Mexican boxer and former world champion in four weight divisions.

JUDGES—The three people scoring boxing matches at ringside.

JUNIOR OLYMPICS—National competition for boxers ages 8 to 16 that can lead to a spot on a future USA Olympic boxing team.

JUNIOR WITTER—English boxer and former world champion in two weight divisions.

K

KNOCKDOWN—When a boxer hits hard enough that the opponent drops to the canvas completely or onto one knee. If he or she doesn't stand up by the count of 10, it is a knockout.

KNOCKOUT—When a boxer hits so hard that the opponent either loses consciousness or is unable to stand up within 10 seconds.

L

LARRY HOLMES—Longtime world heavyweight boxing champion.

M

MAJORITY DECISION—Two of the three judges agree that one fighter won and the third judge scores it a tie.

MAKING WEIGHT—Boxers fight in one of 18 weight classes. (See *Weight Class*.) Making weight refers to the most they may weigh in order to fight in a certain class.

MANAGER—Person who runs a boxer's business. The manager negotiates what the boxer is paid for a bout, hires a trainer, arranges travel, and performs other duties.

MANNY PACQUIAO—Philippine world champion boxer in eight weight divisions and sitting Filipino senator.

MATCH SCORING—Points awarded during a bout. Each judge gives 10 points to the winner of a round, and nine points to the opponent. If a fighter is knocked down or assessed a penalty by the referee, he or she might get only eight points for the round. In a 12-round bout, if one fighter wins eight rounds and the other wins four, the match score is 116-112.

MEDICINE BALL—Heavy ball about twice the size and shape of a basketball. Boxers gain strength in training by throwing it back and forth.

MGM GRAND GARDEN ARENA—Venue in Las Vegas famous for staging major prize fights.

MICHAEL BUFFER—Boxing ring announcer known for his flashy fighter introductions and decision announcements.

MUHAMMAD ALI—Legendary heavyweight boxing champion and humanitarian.

O

ODDS—Betting numbers casinos use to describe the relative strength of boxers, and to attract gamblers. If one fighter is favored over the other by 6-1 odds, the casino believes he or she is about six times more likely to win than the other.

P

PAY-PER-VIEW—Special cable TV programming available for a one-time fee. Championship prizefights often are broadcast on pay-per-view for costs ranging from $30 to $100.

POWER PUNCH—Any punch other than a jab.

PRESS ROW—Area where media people (writers and broadcasters) sit to cover a boxing match near the ring.

PRIZEFIGHT—Professional boxing match for which the fighters receive pay.

PROMOTER—Person or company that puts on fights. The promoter negotiates payment with the fighters' mangers, rents an arena, publicizes the match, and takes a most of the financial risk.

PURSE—Fee prizefighters earn from the promoter for a single match.

R

REFEREE—Person in the ring with the boxers who rules on illegal fighting, does the count when a fighter is knocked down, and can stop a fight if a fighter appears to be in danger of being badly injured.

REMATCH—Repeat bout. A rematch is a losing fighter's chance to even the score. The right to a rematch is often in fighters' contracts for a fight.

RING ANNOUNCER—Person who introduces the fighters before the match and who announces the decision at the end.

RING DOCTOR—Physician who examines boxers during matches and can stop the fight if he or she deems an injury severe enough.

RUBBER MATCH—Third match between two boxers who each have won one of the previous bouts.

RUBBERY LEGS—Instability of a fighter when he or she is in trouble from being punched and may be about to be knocked out. Usually, when a referee sees rubbery legs, he stops the fight.

ROCKY BALBOA—Fictional heavyweight prizefighter featured in the "Rocky" movies

RUSLAN PROVODNIKOV—Russian prizefighter known as "The Siberian Brawler" for his wild punching style.

S

SANCTIONING ORGANIZATION—One of the groups that award championship boxing titles. There are four main sanctioning organizations: the International Boxing Federation, the World Boxing Association, the World Boxing Council, and the World Boxing Organization.

SLAP GLOVES—Hand-eye coordination boxers learn by hitting each other's open hands usually supervised by their trainers.

SLIPPING A PUNCH—Ducking or avoiding an opponent's punch.

SPARRING PARTNER—Practice boxer who helps prepare a fighter for an upcoming match by going a few rounds against him in training. Sparring boxers always wear headgear. Sometimes, sparring partners go on to become famous on their own.

SPEED BAG—Equipment in a boxing gym about the size and shape of a basketball hung from a platform above the boxer, who hits it repeatedly to start constant, unpredictable movement to train hand and foot speed.

SPLIT DECISION—Two judges rule that one fighter has won and the third judge gives it to the other fighter.

SUGAR RAY LEONARD—U.S. Olympic boxing and world champion in five weight divisions.

SWEET SCIENCE—Nickname for the sport of boxing.

T

TECHNICAL KNOCKOUT—TKO, when the referee or ring doctor rules that one fighter cannot continue. The other fighter is credited with a TKO.

TEDDY ATLAS—Famous boxing training and TV commentator.

TITLE DEFENSE—Boxing champion must give other boxers a chance to win the title. When he or she does, it is called a title defense.

TRAINER—Boxer's coach and his corner boss during a match.

TRILOGY—Three fights between the same boxers. If each has won one, the third is a rubber match.

U

UNDERCARD—Fights that precede the main event. On a big fight night, there might be as many as seven fights before the main event.

UNANIMOUS DECISION—All three judges score the fight for the same boxer.

UPPERCUT—Boxing punch thrown with the elbow held close to the body.

W

WEIGH-IN—Boxers are weighed the day before a match to ensure they do not exceed the limit for their weight class.

WEIGHT CLASS—Professional boxing has 18 weight classes, ranging from light minimumweight (102 pounds) to heavyweight (no upper limit).

WORLD BOXING ASSOCIATION—WBA, a sanctioning group.

WORLD BOXING COUNCIL—WBC, a sanctioning group.

WORLD BOXING ORGANIZATION—WBO, a sanctioning group.

CPSIA information can be obtained
at www.ICGtesting.com
Printed in the USA
FSOW03n1047161117
41281FS